HOME AND FAMILY

Learn Italian with Puzzles

Italian Language Learning Puzzle Book (Vol 2)

Play Italian

Books by Play Italian

- Travel to Italy – Learn Italian with Puzzles
- Home and Family – Learn Italian with Puzzles

HOW TO USE THIS BOOK

Thank you for buying a copy of *Home and Family*, the second in a series of puzzle books aimed at Italian language students. The idea is to have fun while you pick up some new Italian vocabulary, specifically around the theme of home and family life.

For instance, you will be able to learn new words about family relationships, various rooms in the house, cooking and eating and spending time with your loved ones.

This book includes:

- 32 word searches

- 20 freeform crosswords

- 12 word fit puzzles

- 16 word matches

- 10 word scrambles

- 10 cryptograms

The puzzles are designed to help beginners pick up new words, or intermediate students to brush up their Italian knowledge. As I wanted the puzzles to be fun and challenging for both levels, I have structured the book the following way:

Word Searches

The word searches have Italian words that you need to find in the grid. Words can go in any direction: left to right, right to left, top to bottom, bottom to top, diagonally up or down.

The majority of word searches comes in two versions: *a* and *b*.

Version *a*, the more challenging one (ideal for intermediate students), has the words in Italian inside the grid, but in English below the grid. This means that you have to translate the English words into Italian first, before finding them within the grid. Version *b*, (ideal for beginner students) has the words in Italian both inside the grid and below the grid.

For extra fun, even though version *b* has the same Italian words inside the grid as version *a*, these word are located in different places within the grid, so it will feel like you're solving two different puzzles.

Freeform Crosswords

The freeform crosswords have the clues in Italian, but there is also a Help section in the book, on page 124, with the clues in English, for those who struggle to understand the Italian clues. The clues in English are not necessarily a literal translation of the Italian clues.

Word Fit Puzzles

These can work well for both beginners and intermediate students, as it's about placing the words correctly within the grid.
I recommend you start with letter sizes that have the fewest words. So if there are only 2 words with 5 letters and 6 words with 4 letters, try placing the 5 letter words first.

Word Scrambles

These are lists of words that have been scrambled, and your task is to place the letters in the correct order. As these can be particularly challenging, they are designed in two varieties: an easier one, where some letters are suggested, and a trickier one, with no help.

Cryptograms

These are usually quotes from someone famous. To stay within this book's overall theme, the quotes are related to the topic of life at home and with the family.

Your task is to replace the numbers in the puzzle with the correct letters, and reveal the quote.

For these you have the option of using some of the hints provided, or just try to complete the activity without the help.

These may be easier to complete for a student of Italian at intermediate level, but even if you're a beginner, why not try?

Word Matches

These come in two types. The first one is about matching Italian words to English words, so it's a straightforward translation activity. The second one is about matching Italian words to other Italian words (by context). The latter is probably more suitable for intermediate level students, but again, if you're a beginner, it's worth a try, perhaps with the help of an Italian dictionary.

Solutions

All solutions are provided at the end of the book. For easier reference, the solutions are grouped by puzzle type. So you will find all the word search solutions first, then all the crossword solutions, and so on.

And finally...

A little about me. My name is Martina and I was born and brought up in Italy. I am passionate about languages, and having fun while learning.

This is the second puzzle book I created for Italian language learners.

I also have a website with plenty of resources, puzzles and games. Some you can download, print and solve at home, some you can play online. You can also subscribe to my monthly newsletter and receive free puzzles and fun Italian learning resources.

Go on... have a look at *playitalian.com* and do let me know how you get on.

Ciao for now

Martina

Translate the English words below the grid into Italian and find them in the Word Search. If this is too challenging, please turn the page for an easier puzzle.

```
J V B A R Q R C F N G X U M B
O N I R D A P I U D U D A C D
U N S D E P G W P E R D A P G
P O N D O L L E T A R F I N M
I R O T I N E G L E G Z U G L
N E N O C S S J K E T O P I N
Z C N N C N C G N L R O V S W
U O O N O K O E R A T T O D A
C U T O I Z R T N U H R T M N
B S A N L O Y N U D E H A E I
F O N I G U C E E L E B N J R
C B G U I A V R L X O N E Q D
G B O L F K S A M M A M T C A
Q A C N C P I P T B E S N E M
N B O E Y Y H Q F N E F A X D
```

TO ADOPT	GODSON	GRANDFATHER
ANCESTOR	BROTHER	DAUGTHER-IN-LAW
DAD	SON-IN-LAW	FATHER
GREAT-GRANDFATHER	PARENTS	GODFATHER
BROTHER-IN-LAW	MOTHER	RELATIVE
COUSIN	GODMOTHER	SISTER
DESCENDANT	MUM	FATHER-IN-LAW
SON	NEPHEW	UNCLE

La famiglia

Find the Italian words below the grid in the Word Search puzzle. These are the same
Italian words as in 1a, but they're located in different positions on the grid.

```
W  S  P  O  D  J  L  U  Y  O  C  D  P  N  H
R  I  A  L  I  R  O  T  I  N  E  G  V  G  A
M  X  D  L  S  C  Y  A  Z  N  A  W  I  P  M
R  X  R  E  C  N  C  Q  T  O  R  S  U  K  O
R  P  E  T  E  C  N  O  N  N  O  N  S  I  B
A  O  T  A  N  G  O  C  I  R  U  K  O  P  B
O  N  I  R  D  A  P  C  E  L  N  E  A  M  A
R  I  V  F  E  C  P  L  M  J  G  R  N  A  B
E  G  Z  V  N  V  L  Y  V  L  E  I  M  D  C
C  U  Q  O  T  A  N  E  T  N  A  A  F  R  B
O  C  A  I  E  R  A  T  T  O  D  A  J  E  T
U  Z  C  L  B  O  N  E  O  R  E  N  E  G  W
S  T  X  G  E  T  O  P  I  N  Z  S  S  T  Z
C  J  W  I  V  D  T  N  T  D  D  D  B  S  R
Y  I  H  F  B  N  A  M  M  A  M  C  D  H  L
```

ADOTTARE	FIGLIOCCIO	NONNO
ANTENATO	FRATELLO	NUORA
BABBO	GENERO	PADRE
BISNONNO	GENITORI	PADRINO
COGNATO	MADRE	PARENTE
CUGINO	MADRINA	SORELLA
DISCENDENTE	MAMMA	SUOCERO
FIGLIO	NIPOTE	ZIO

Salutarsi

Translate the English words below the grid into Italian and find them in the Word Search. If this is too challenging, please turn the page for an easier puzzle.

```
C M M T C T S E M I R C A L Q
V K G G U M O R T N O C N I M
J K O O I C C A R B B A W G X
Q I S S A N G T O O Y D I S B
T S I M E S E N O I Z O M E T
A R R I V E D E R C I L N O V
R E R S L T R S C A U T G W C
E T O R A T Z E X B O I D D A
S T S A S O N R I R A P E P Q
A A H D G N F P N L J G H U O
N B M E O A B A Y G G F E Q A
O M W G I N T R M U G O A I C
U I O N R O I G N O U B C Q R
B C N O T U N E V N E B U C Y
T S L C I B Q X R W M K G L A
```

HUG	GOODNIGHT	JOY
TO WELCOME	GOOD EVENING	ENCOUNTER
FAREWELL	GOOD MORNING	TO COME ACROSS
GOODBYE	TO LEAVE	TEARS
KISS	GESTURE	TO INTRODUCE
WELCOME BACK	HELLO (1)	HELLO (2)
WELCOME	EMOTION	SMILE

Salutarsi

Find the Italian words below the grid in the Word Search puzzle. These are the same Italian words as in 2a, but they're located in different positions on the grid.

```
A O H O T U N E V N E B U P H
R R X M O S I R R O S C E H M
E T R N H I U A I O I G O H X
S N M I S R E T T A B M I W O
A O W S V U R N O Q F K C P T
N C K R S E R E I L G O C C A
O N O A Z T D S C O O N A B N
U I L D R T A E U P E R R Y R
B V N E C O N R R M E O B L O
E O Y G Z N B P O C M I B V T
M O K N O A O Z I K I G A L N
Z N C O L N I R C D R N Y C E
J A W C J O D N A P C O S L B
V H O F N U D I B J A U K K H
V S O E K B A X A Z L B E N O
```

ABBRACCIO	BUONANOTTE	GIOIA
ACCOGLIERE	BUONASERA	INCONTRO
ADDIO	BUONGIORNO	IMBATTERSI
ARRIVEDERCI	CONGEDARSI	LACRIME
BACIO	CENNO	PRESENTARE
BENTORNATO	CIAO	SALVE
BENVENUTO	EMOZIONE	SORRISO

Translate the English words below the grid into Italian and find them in the Word Search. If this is too challenging, please turn the page for an easier puzzle.

```
P X U Z D E C O R A Z I O N I
F W A A E T T I S I D N I R B
U O T I V N I R N R T I T H E
Y O R T S A N E B O K C N X L
I G O I K M P D Q D F N E Y N
G A T P U U A I M L M O R N E
Z I I S F P T S G A U L A P S
O H I O W S I E E B E L P B B
L C E D I S C D L R S A O B L
A O V O R G S F E Z P P D H Z
G I R U G U A E D I E R R A T
E G C G J T N S N G G I O T U
R B X L E M R A A T A D C S G
H F F L O X N I C I M A I E W
C L Y V I D F R F B M K R F Y
```

FRIENDS	SWEETS	GUESTS
BEST WISHES	PARTY	BALLOONS
NOISY FUN	GAMES	RELATIVES
TOAST	JOY	GIFT
CANDLES	INVITATION	MEMORY
DATE	MUSIC	SURPRISE
WISH	BIRTH	SPARKLING WINE
DECORATIONS	RIBBON	CAKE

La festa di compleanno

Find the Italian words below the grid in the Word Search puzzle. These are the same Italian words as in 3a, but they're located in different positions on the grid.

```
M  I  H  D  S  A  I  O  I  G  Z  M  T  D  T
O  I  U  P  T  R  P  H  J  I  C  I  M  A  F
B  G  J  S  I  T  N  E  R  A  P  C  X  G  X
Q  C  E  A  S  E  R  P  R  O  S  L  I  M  O
D  F  A  T  I  C  S  A  N  Y  I  O  R  N  H
W  E  L  E  D  N  A  C  J  X  C  D  U  X  E
L  T  C  A  N  A  Y  O  P  H  E  M  G  D  A
M  N  T  O  I  R  E  D  I  S  E  D  U  O  M
L  A  M  D  R  M  U  F  E  C  K  J  A  N  P
N  M  X  R  B  A  I  R  O  D  L  A  B  U  U
G  U  H  O  L  N  Z  K  S  U  K  V  J  G  M
R  P  F  C  V  I  N  I  C  N  O  L  L  A  P
L  S  T  I  T  I  P  S  O  R  T  S  A  N  P
Q  A  T  R  O  T  Y  C  N  N  W  B  M  R  F
U  O  L  A  G  E  R  M  A  C  I  S  U  M  V
```

AMICI	DOLCI	OSPITI
AUGURI	FESTA	PALLONCINI
BALDORIA	GIOCHI	PARENTI
BRINDISI	GIOIA	REGALO
CANDELE	INVITO	RICORDO
DATA	MUSICA	SORPRESA
DESIDERIO	NASCITA	SPUMANTE
DECORAZIONI	NASTRO	TORTA

Un neonato in casa

This freeform crossword has the clues in Italian. If you struggle to understand some of the clues, you can find them in English in the *Help Section* on page 124

Orizzontali

2. Una sedia col vassoio

3. Gesti di tenerezza e amore

7. Concede una pausa ai genitori

11. Il letto del bebè

12. Dove cambi il bebè

13. La bottiglia da succhiare

14. La neo-mamma ne perde tanto

Verticali

1. Fanno male alla pancino

4. Dà conforto al neonato

5. Ti fa portare a spasso il bebè

6. Svegliano i genitori

8. Giocattolo soffice

9. Bisogna cambiarlo spesso

10. Si lega intorno al collo

Facciamo colazione

This freeform crossword has the clues in Italian. If you struggle to understand some of the clues, you can find them in English in the *Help Section* on page 124

Orizzontali

4. C'è alla frutta e naturale
7. Emette un buffo rumore
8. È più buona quando è di stagione
10. Il caffè con la spuma
12. Frutta che si può spalmare
13. Lo usi per pulirti le labbra
14. Sono dolci e di varie forme

Verticali

1. È bianco e si beve a tutte le età
2. Meno calorico dello zucchero
3. Serve a mescolare lo zucchero
5. Lo producono le api
6. Si usa per bere il tè
9. Il più famoso è alla crema
11. Si mescolano con il latte

Festa della mamma e del papà

Match the Italian words on the left, to the English words on the right.

biglietto	son
fiori	daughter
regalo	family
domenica	photo
ricordi	present
figlio	memories
figlia	Sunday
brindisi	fondness
festa	toast
affetto	card
famiglia	celebration
fotografia	flowers

Leggiamo il giornale

Match the Italian words on the left, to the English words on the right.

titolo	journalist
articolo	page
pagina	press
fotografia	headline
rubrica	photo
notizie	interview
pubblicità	cartoon
vignetta	news
edicola	article
intervista	advert
stampa	column
giornalista	newsagent's

I nonni

Below this Word Fit puzzle there is a list of words.
Place the words correctly into the grid.

7 lettere
Affetto
Anziani
Coccole
Materni
Passato
Paterni
Ricordi

8 lettere
Occhiali
Pazienza
Pensione

9 lettere
Abitudini
Vecchiaia

10 lettere
Disciplina
Esperienza

Tipi di abitazione

Below this Word Fit puzzle there is a list of words.
Place the words correctly into the grid.

4 lettere	**6 lettere**	**8 lettere**	**10 lettere**
Casa	Trullo	Bungalow	Monolocale
		Castello	
5 lettere	**7 lettere**	Fattoria	**11 lettere**
Baita	Capanna	Roulotte	Grattacielo
Villa	Palazzo		
	Rifugio		**12 lettere**
			Appartamento

10   Quote by Oliver Wendell Holmes Sr.

Replace the numbers in the grid with the correct letters, and reveal the quote.

Hints: 26 = A   9 = L   16 = 0   21 = T

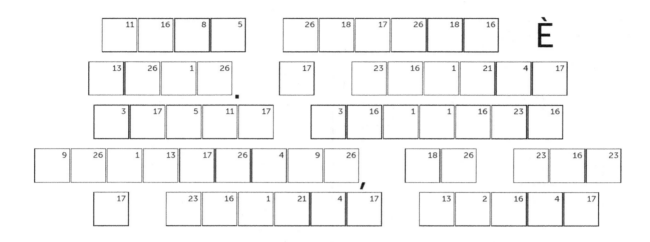

11   Quote by Christian Morgenstern

Replace the numbers in the grid with the correct letters, and reveal the quote.

Hints: 24 = C   13 = D   21 = O   4 = V

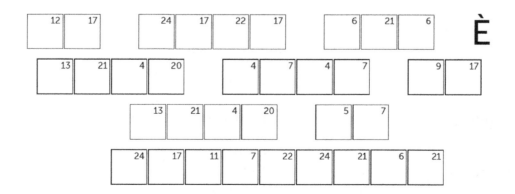

Il ricettario

The following words have been scrambled. Place the letters in the correct order.
For a less challenging version of this puzzle, please turn the page.

IINOOPZR   _ _ _ _ _ _ _ _

ENIIGTDIENR   _ _ _ _ _ _ _ _ _ _ _

OCDIEMINNT   _ _ _ _ _ _ _ _ _

ZINTRSOUII   _ _ _ _ _ _ _ _ _

UTORACT   _ _ _ _ _ _ _

ENICID   _ _ _ _ _ _

TETRIAC   _ _ _ _ _ _ _

MTIEP   _ _ _ _ _

MIAMINGI   _ _ _ _ _ _ _ _

OLCEARI   _ _ _ _ _ _ _

RAUTEATEPMR   _ _ _ _ _ _ _ _ _ _ _

EPSO   _ _ _ _

Il ricettario

The words on the left have been scrambled. Place the letters in the correct order.

IINOOPZR   P _ _ Z _ _ _ I

ENIIGTDIENR   I _ _ _ _ D _ _ _ _ I

OCDIEMINNT   C _ _ _ _ M _ _ _ I

ZINTRSOUII   I _ _ _ U _ _ _ _ I

UTORACT   C _ _ _ _ _ A

ENICID   I _ _ _ _ E

TETRIAC   R _ _ _ _ _ A

MTIEP   T _ _ _ I

MIAMINGI   I _ _ _ G _ _ I

OLCEARI   C _ _ _ _ _ E

RAUTEATEPMR   T _ _ _ _ R _ _ _ _ A

EPSO   P _ _ _

Translate the English words below the grid into Italian and find them in the Word Search. If this is too challenging, please turn the page for an easier puzzle.

```
R P E Z N O E L A F F A C S S
I P Z W Z O N I Z Z A G A M B
U Q Y F Q V R V G F A T S A P
Y O G C P E A I W G P V S T H
N S N H M H C S X A A S A S D
R I M U G E L R N M O M C U O
M R L O B I C E A C L T R B S
A A I N I C I T T A L T L O W
S J E I F B J E T R E F F O F
E N R R P P X D U R R D F N K
P N U T P D R G R E R U H I R
S E D N A V E B F Y A G X T C
D J R O S S E M M O C T O S B
N E E C S E P V G F R U Y E A
Y S V S K F O Y G Z Z I K C N
```

DRINKS	DETERGENTS	PASTA
SHOPPING BAG	CHEESE (plural)	FISH
MEAT	FRUIT	RICE
TROLLEY	DAIRY PRODUCTS	DELI COUNTER
TILL	PULSES	SHELF
BASKET	WAREHOUSE	RECEIPT
FOOD	OFFERS	GROCERIES
SHOP ASSISTANT	BREAD	VEGETABLES

Al supermercato

Find the Italian words below the grid in the Word Search puzzle. These are the same Italian words as in 13a, but they're located in different positions on the grid.

```
E  R  U  D  R  E  V  C  A  S  S  A  C  Y  P
D  G  D  G  Z  U  H  N  C  U  P  Y  M  M  F
N  E  C  S  E  P  V  O  B  E  N  A  P  Z  Q
A  T  T  U  R  F  N  V  C  L  G  I  B  T  P
V  R  V  E  L  T  I  G  G  A  M  R  O  F  P
E  E  S  N  R  G  I  A  Z  F  H  E  S  V  A
B  F  Z  I  Z  S  N  Z  Y  F  Q  M  S  H  X
G  F  N  L  G  H  I  F  A  A  J  U  E  O  D
B  O  B  I  C  N  C  V  W  C  A  L  M  W  D
K  N  B  F  O  C  I  A  I  S  O  A  M  K  R
Q  I  G  G  A  A  T  N  M  M  S  S  O  T  X
N  T  G  R  T  A  T  S  U  B  I  P  C  W  L
R  S  N  T  S  P  A  R  G  V  R  L  E  J  U
B  E  B  P  A  O  L  L  E  R  R  A  C  S  L
K  C  A  L  P  S  P  Y  L  T  Y  F  P  G  A
```

BEVANDE	DETERSIVI	PASTA
BUSTA	FORMAGGI	PESCE
CARNE	FRUTTA	RISO
CARRELLO	LATTICINI	SALUMERIA
CASSA	LEGUMI	SCAFFALE
CESTINO	MAGAZZINO	SCONTRINO
CIBO	OFFERTE	SPESA
COMMESSO	PANE	VERDURE

Translate the English words below the grid into Italian and find them in the Word Search. If this is too challenging, please turn the page for an easier puzzle.

```
R G H U S A K A L U O X B C R
C Z H K J R T Y L J P M A Q Q
Q E N O T T E N A P E N N C D
E N L R P W J R X R T R E G E
M I K E R B M E C I D U C O O
F L L B B R U A R E T T E L L
K L F L C R T C A N D E L A A
W A I A E I A D N A L R I H G
M P L I N O I Z A R O C E D E
E Z N O O T T A I C U L P I R
E V E N R I F L W O S E E B J
H X G E R R O L E G N A S E S
N K N U O I I E B G W E E G Y
K N G X T P Y T V F K F R V R
A T T I L S A S S E M L P I Q
```

TREE	DECEMBER	PANETTONE
ANGEL	WREATH	NATIVITY SCENE
STOCKINGS	LETTER	PRESENT
CANDLE	LIGHTS	REINDEER
CAROLS	STREET MARKET	SLEDGE
CELEBRATION	MASS	SPIRIT
DINNER	SNOW	STAR
DECORATIONS	BAUBLES	NOUGAT

Natale

Find the Italian words below the grid in the Word Search puzzle. These are the same
Italian words as in 14a, but they're located in different positions on the grid.

```
H A E Q O O W M F A I C U L Z
I I S V R D T L H Q A N E C X
A A N N E R E N I L L A P O C
N A X W B N N R Z U U S E J N
A T T I L S O E B P V S S S G
L S E N A H T S G M Q E E Z D
L K C O N I T A C R E M R A O
E K I I O L E G N A C C P L L
T I X Z K E N O R R O T I E A
S C C A D N A L R I H G T D G
J G P R R T P Z S S C T N N E
S W M O T I R I P S E J A A R
M Q M C L O E P K R G A C C K
R L C E L E B R A Z I O N E Q
P T L D W Y L N L M R B L H Z
```

ALBERO	DICEMBRE	PANETTONE
ANGELO	GHIRLANDA	PRESEPE
CALZE	LETTERA	REGALO
CANDELA	LUCI	RENNA
CANTI	MERCATINO	SLITTA
CELEBRAZIONE	MESSA	SPIRITO
CENA	NEVE	STELLA
DECORAZIONI	PALLINE	TORRONE

Translate the English words below the grid into Italian and find them in the Word Search. If this is too challenging, please turn the page for an easier puzzle.

```
T  E  Y  M  H  A  H  W  V  L  D  M  T  E  Z
O  E  L  L  E  N  O  T  T  A  M  J  O  U  Q
H  A  R  E  I  H  G  N  I  R  E  J  Z  V  Q
V  J  A  M  A  S  J  A  T  R  O  P  G  D  M
E  Q  N  G  O  S  S  E  R  G  N  I  E  A  H
Y  E  L  A  C  S  B  O  N  A  I  P  N  N  I
P  O  L  O  N  G  I  M  O  C  M  S  O  I  Z
W  L  L  O  C  R  R  F  I  A  A  R  C  T  J
Z  L  Z  T  I  L  U  X  O  R  C  R  L  N  U
Y  E  A  T  N  E  M  A  D  N  O  F  A  A  Q
R  C  Z  I  I  L  F  A  I  X  I  V  B  C  V
T  N  N  F  D  O  U  E  R  T  S  E  N  I  F
G  A  A  F  A  G  P  O  R  T  S  A  L  I  P
Z  C  T  O  R  E  I  N  O  T  T  A  M  J  B
D  G  S  S  G  T  W  O  C  T  E  T  T  O  Y
```

BALCONY	STEPS	DOOR
FIREPLACE	ENTRANCE	BANISTER
GATE	LOFT	STAIRS
CELLAR	BRICKS	CEILING
CHIMNEY	TILES	ROOM
CORRIDOR	WALLS	ROOF TILES
WINDOWS	FLOOR	RADIATORS
FOUNDATIONS	PILLAR	ROOF

La casa

Find the Italian words below the grid in the Word Search puzzle. These are the same Italian words as in 15a, but they're located in different positions on the grid.

```
T  A  E  A  T  N  E  M  A  D  N  O  F  K  V
F  M  D  R  T  E  L  L  E  N  O  T  T  A  M
Z  Y  X  E  D  O  R  T  S  A  L  I  P  D  G
V  O  N  I  M  A  C  M  P  E  O  U  L  R  B
L  U  H  H  O  W  J  I  O  V  N  A  A  A  W
E  L  O  G  E  T  A  Z  I  S  G  D  E  S  K
L  E  L  N  P  N  H  M  O  Z  I  J  C  N  T
A  T  L  I  O  O  V  A  D  N  M  F  J  A  S
C  J  E  R  T  S  E  N  I  F  O  A  O  M  J
S  Z  C  J  T  S  E  I  R  E  C  Z  Z  N  S
O  D  N  L  I  E  A  T  R  O  P  N  K  A  I
F  E  A  U  F  R  E  N  O  C  L  A  B  P  V
J  M  C  Y  F  G  J  A  C  V  O  T  T  E  T
M  U  R  I  O  N  I  C  Q  R  V  S  V  R  S
I  Q  L  P  S  I  N  O  T  T  A  M  E  N  J
```

BALCONE	GRADINI	PORTA
CAMINO	INGRESSO	RINGHIERA
CANCELLO	MANSARDA	SCALE
CANTINA	MATTONI	SOFFITTO
COMIGNOLO	MATTONELLE	STANZA
CORRIDOIO	MURI	TEGOLE
FINESTRE	PIANO	TERMOSIFONI
FONDAMENTA	PILASTRO	TETTO

Spaghetti al pomodoro

This freeform crossword has the clues in Italian. If you struggle to understand some of the clues, you can find them in English in the *Help Section* on page 125

Orizzontali

4. È più breve se ti piacciono al dente
5. Si fa bollire per alcuni minuti
6. Dove si serve la pasta
8. Lo grattugi sul piatto
10. Dà un profumo al sugo
11. Se manca sono insipidi

Verticali

1. Utensile con tanti buchi
2. Si arrotolano nella forchetta
3. Son più buoni se freschi
5. Si fa soffriggere per un gusto deciso
6. Si usa per cucinare la pasta
7. Il migliore è quello d'oliva
9. Si usa per mescolare

Bricolage/Fai da te

This freeform crossword has the clues in Italian. If you struggle to understand some of the clues, you can find them in English in the *Help Section* on page 125

Orizzontali

3. Afferra viti e bulloni
4. Ha i gradini ed è trasportabile
6. Perfetta per tagliare il legno
8. Fa prendere le giuste misure
10. Viene battuto dal martello
11. Serve per fare buchi
12. Indica se la superficie è orizzontale

Verticali

1. Funziona solo se lo ruoti
2. Copre e protegge i mobili
4. Necessaria per stuccare
5. Attrezzo per verniciare
7. Fa ruotare dadi e bulloni
9. Lampada portatile
10. Fa attaccare due oggetti insieme

Hobby

Match the Italian words on the left, to the Italian words on the right.

lettura	rastrello
pittura	cruciverba
ricamo	scacchiera
astronomia	ricettario
giardinaggio	ferri
scacchi	musica
filatelia	telescopio
magia	pennello
cucina	francobolli
maglia	libro
enigmistica	bacchetta
danza	ago

Attrezzi vari della casa

Match the Italian words on the left, to the Italian words on the right.

cacciavite	tagliare
metro	strofinare
forbici	spalare
trapano	verniciare
torcia	battere
martello	asciugare
pennello	spazzare
ferro	illuminare
phon	misurare
scopa	avvitare
pala	stirare
spazzola	perforare

Addio al nubilato/celibato

Below this Word Fit puzzle there is a list of words.
Place the words correctly into the grid.

5 lettere	7 lettere	9 lettere	10 lettere
Amici	Sbornia	Fidanzati	Palloncini
Festa	Scherzi	Discoteca	
Sposi		Testimoni	12 lettere
	8 lettere		Divertimento
6 lettere	Brindisi		
Serata	Invitati		
Giochi			

This freeform crossword has the clues in Italian. If you struggle to understand some of the clues, you can find them in English in the *Help Section* on page 125

Orizzontali

3. Proteggono dal sole e dalla pioggia
5. Quella di Trevi è famosa
8. È tanto nelle ore di punta
9. Sono soliti a fine stagione
11. Dove si fa shopping
12. Ci si prende un caffè
13. È pieno di bancarelle

Verticali

1. È affollata in un giorno caldo
2. Necessario se vuoi fare acquisti
3. Perfetta per riposarsi un po'
4. Ci camminano i pedoni
6. Spesso vi si espone la merce
7. Trasporta molte persone
10. Spesso è abbellita da un monumento

22 Quote by Michel de Montaigne

Replace the numbers in the grid with the correct letters, and reveal the quote.

Hints: 6 = E   21 = F   1 = O   9 = R

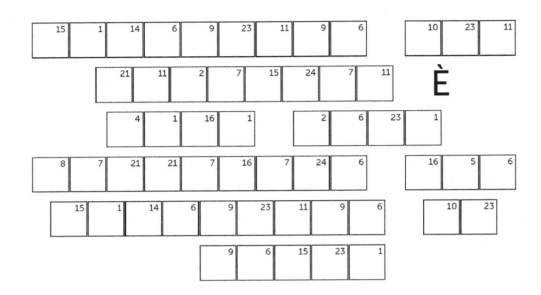

23 Quote Johann Wolfgang von Goethe

Replace the numbers in the grid with the correct letters, and reveal the quote.

Hints: 1 = A   25 = C   17 = F   19 = L

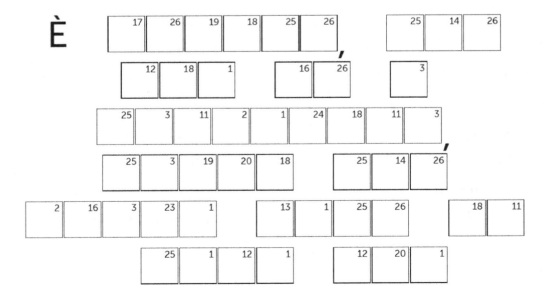

I compiti di matematica

The following words have been scrambled. Place the letters in the correct order.
For a less challenging version of this puzzle, please turn the page.

NTLBELIEA   _ _ _ _ _ _ _ _ _

ZINEDIDAO   _ _ _ _ _ _ _ _ _

IVNIOIDES   _ _ _ _ _ _ _ _ _

OEISATTONRZ   _ _ _ _ _ _ _ _ _ _ _

RNPECAETLUE   _ _ _ _ _ _ _ _ _ _ _

ZENAROIF   _ _ _ _ _ _ _ _

AEMCIDIL   _ _ _ _ _ _ _ _

TMIIECARAT   _ _ _ _ _ _ _ _ _ _

UOMERN   _ _ _ _ _ _

UASIRM   _ _ _ _ _ _

ILTLMOUP   _ _ _ _ _ _ _ _

OTGEAERIM   _ _ _ _ _ _ _ _ _

I compiti di matematica

The words on the left have been scrambled. Place the letters in the correct order.

NTLBELIEA   T _ _ _ L _ _ _ E

ZINEDIDAO   A _ _ _ Z _ _ _ E

IVNIOIDES   D _ _ _ S _ _ _ E

OEISATTONRZ   S _ _ _ R _ _ _ _ _ E

RNPECAETLUE   P _ _ _ _ N _ _ _ _ E

ZENAROIF   F _ _ Z _ _ _ E

AEMCIDIL   D _ _ _ M _ _ I

TMIIECARAT   A _ _ _ M _ _ _ _ A

UOMERN   N _ _ _ _ O

UASIRM   M _ _ _ _ A

ILTLMOUP   M _ _ T _ _ _ O

OTGEAERIM   G _ _ _ E _ _ _ A

La cucina

Translate the English words below the grid into Italian and find them in the Word Search. If this is too challenging, please turn the page for an easier puzzle.

```
O  N  R  O  F  Y  O  I  G  O  L  O  R  O  R
I  N  X  V  L  U  S  U  S  M  A  L  Z  Z  U
D  E  D  N  O  O  R  C  I  M  V  O  K  D  B
A  R  E  I  M  U  T  T  A  P  A  V  Y  A  I
R  O  N  I  T  E  P  P  A  T  S  A  I  L  N
E  T  N  O  T  T  R  G  A  I  T  T  I  O  E
C  A  O  I  C  C  A  N  I  F  O  R  T  S  T
I  L  I  R  H  G  C  I  N  P  V  R  T  N  T
L  L  U  A  A  S  N  E  P  S  I  D  E  E  O
L  U  T  T  O  L  L  E  B  A  G  S  S  M  G
E  R  O  T  A  R  I  P  S  A  L  T  S  B  I
N  F  J  E  I  D  E  S  T  W  I  O  A  Q  R
R  S  A  C  S  A  Z  N  E  D  E  R  C  N  F
O  O  N  I  D  N  A  V  A  L  S  C  D  S  Z
F  R  Y  R  V  E  T  R  I  N  A  E  H  R  O
```

EXTRACTOR FAN	SINK	TAP/FAUCET
DRAWERS	DISHWASHER	CHAIRS
CUPBOARD	SHELF	STOOL
PANTRY	MICROWAVE	DISH DRAINER
COOKER/STOVE	CLOCK	TEA TOWEL
OVEN	DUSTBIN	RUG/MAT
FRIDGE	RADIO	TABLE
BLENDER	COOKBOOK	GLASS CABINET

La cucina

Find the Italian words below the grid in the Word Search puzzle. These are the same Italian words as in 25a, but they're located in different positions on the grid.

```
V W S G A B E L L O Z U O E E
E O N I D N A V A L O G I R F
T E D N O O R C I M I L C O I
R A Z N E D E R C P G K C T Q
I S O M O R I L O I O Z A A Y
N N N E N A M T V T L O N R F
A E I I R L U O J T O T I I O
S P T O O O T I O A R T F P R
X S E L F S T D B I O E O S N
H I P O A N A A I P G N R A E
V D P V S E P R L A R I T I L
E Q A A B M W L E L G B S M L
T L T T S E D I E O U U D Y I
F M O I R A T T E C I R W X M
Z C V S I T T E S S A C F U H
```

ASPIRATORE	LAVANDINO	RUBINETTO
CASSETTI	LAVASTOVIGLIE	SEDIE
CREDENZA	MENSOLA	SGABELLO
DISPENSA	MICROONDE	SCOLAPIATTI
FORNELLI	OROLOGIO	STROFINACCIO
FORNO	PATTUMIERA	TAPPETINO
FRIGO	RADIO	TAVOLO
FRULLATORE	RICETTARIO	VETRINA

Translate the English words below the grid into Italian and find them in the Word Search. If this is too challenging, please turn the page for an easier puzzle.

```
P  T  U  H  C  K  K  O  U  T  D  S  T  D  V
E  O  I  C  I  R  F  I  T  N  E  D  Q  A  B
E  B  R  E  T  A  W  G  O  I  Z  V  S  O  C
C  O  O  T  T  E  N  I  B  U  R  C  O  I  D
I  N  A  M  A  G  U  I  C  S  A  O  L  O  S
R  I  I  H  O  B  O  I  H  C  C  E  P  S  W
T  D  C  A  M  U  I  H  C  S  O  N  G  A  B
A  N  C  M  A  W  S  A  I  F  F  U  C  R  S
V  A  O  E  S  N  P  E  N  I  T  T  E  P  C
A  V  D  R  L  P  D  N  P  C  K  Y  U  L  O
L  A  Y  C  A  N  G  U  P  S  H  F  A  T  P
V  L  K  T  B  S  A  P  O  N  E  E  N  E  I
R  O  O  I  R  O  T  U  L  L  O  C  R  D  N
X  I  T  A  P  P  E  T  I  N  O  X  E  I  O
O  N  I  L  O  Z  Z  A  P  S  J  K  N  B  A
```

BATHROBE	TOOTHPASTE	SOAP
TOWELS	SHOWER	TOILET BRUSH
BUBBLE BATH	BASIN	TOOTHBRUSH
CONDITIONER	WASHING MACHINE	MIRROR
BIDET	COMB	SPONGE
CREAM	LAUNDRY BASKET	MAT
MOUTHWASH	SHAVER	BATH/BATHTUB
SHOWER CAP	TAP/FAUCET	TOILET

Il bagno

Find the Italian words below the grid in the Word Search puzzle. These are the same Italian words as in 26a, but they're located in different positions on the grid.

```
C U R E O F O N I P O C S L R
R O A M U I H C S O N G A B A
E I I L N N H M K R I H I S S
M C F O O A E A Y T L Y O D O
A I F I T M N C A A O N M L I
C R U R T A O S F B Z Z A O O
S F C O E G P X V I Z V S N W
A I F T N U A P J A A V L I B
V T E U I I S D A N P Z A T I
Y N N L B C E A D C S W B E D
N E I L U S A I R H C R J P E
B D T O R A N C R E T A W P T
D A T C M O E C I R T A V A L
S P E C C H I O S I O U S T Q
Q Z P X M P N D B A N G U P S
```

ACCAPPATOIO
ASCIUGAMANI
BAGNOSCHIUMA
BALSAMO
BIDET
CREMA
COLLUTORIO
CUFFIA

DENTIFRICIO
DOCCIA
LAVANDINO
LAVATRICE
PETTINE
PORTABIANCHERIA
RASOIO
RUBINETTO

SAPONE
SCOPINO
SPAZZOLINO
SPECCHIO
SPUGNA
TAPPETINO
VASCA
WATER

La camera da letto

Translate the English words below the grid into Italian and find them in the Word Search. If this is too challenging, please turn the page for an easier puzzle.

```
P  Q  J  P  O  I  H  C  C  E  P  S  T  W  I
I  A  G  B  A  I  F  A  R  G  O  T  O  F  L
G  O  R  B  I  L  B  S  A  F  I  I  E  L  H
I  L  W  Y  L  O  C  S  I  O  D  W  L  O  N
A  W  W  L  G  N  T  E  L  T  A  O  O  N  U
M  K  B  S  A  I  M  T  G  T  M  E  F  I  O
A  M  G  T  T  D  O  T  E  E  R  Z  O  C  T
D  Q  X  M  S  N  S  I  V  L  A  W  T  S  T
A  U  Q  V  E  E  S  E  S  C  I  Z  N  U  E
P  A  R  C  V  P  A  R  E  I  P  R  A  C  S
M  D  V  Q  F  P  R  A  E  Z  P  D  P  K  S
A  R  K  Y  S  A  E  N  O  M  U  I  P  O  A
L  O  U  M  E  A  T  R  E  P  O  C  F  B  C
F  E  D  E  R  A  A  L  O  U  Z  N  E  L  X
Z  O  N  I  D  O  M  O  C  T  E  N  D  E  O
```

COAT HANGER	PILLOWCASE	PYJAMAS
WARDROBE	PHOTO	DUVET
CHEST OF DRAWERS	LAMP	PICTURE/PAINTING
DRAWER	SHEETS	SHOE CABINET
BEDSPREAD	BED	ALARM CLOCK
BEDSIDE TABLE	BOOK	MIRROR
BLANKET	MATTRESS	CURTAINS
PILLOW	SLIPPERS	DRESSING GOWN

La camera da letto

Find the Italian words below the grid in the Word Search puzzle. These are the same Italian words as in 27a, but they're located in different positions on the grid.

```
A V W E O Q C L I B R O O F W
R Q R A I F A R G O T O F M W
M E U I H T S A T R E P O C L
A P A L C T S H E D N E T E X
D O F G C O E L O F O T N A P
I I G A E S T P T G M Z H R O
O Q Q T P S T T H U X B U T
L M P S S A I Q E O I P T U T
L H X E D R E S L L P W A W E
D A R V O E R A M A I G I P S
A R M P R T A R E I P R A C S
U E Z P D A O N I D N E P P A
W D V N A M Q O N I D O M O C
O E K G U D N G O N I C S U C
A F J O Q V A I L G E V S K I
```

APPENDINO
ARMADIO
CASSETTIERA
CASSETTO
COPRILETTO
COMODINO
COPERTA
CUSCINO

FEDERA
FOTOGRAFIA
LAMPADA
LENZUOLA
LETTO
LIBRO
MATERASSO
PANTOFOLE

PIGIAMA
PIUMONE
QUADRO
SCARPIERA
SVEGLIA
SPECCHIO
TENDE
VESTAGLIA

Facciamo una torta

This freeform crossword has the clues in Italian. If you struggle to understand some of the clues, you can find them in English in the *Help Section* on page 126

Orizzontali

2. Una sola non basta
6. Si rompono facilmente
7. Le istruzioni da seguire
8. Fa crescere la torta
10. Aiuta a mischiare gli ingredienti
11. Si scioglie facilmente
13. Si accendono per il compleanno

Verticali

1. Rende dolce la torta
3. Vi si versa l'impasto
4. La quantità di un ingrediente
5. Polvere bianca
9. Il recipiente dove prepari l'impasto
10. Deve esser sempre caldo
12. Di solito è montata

Giochi e giocattoli

This freeform crossword has the clues in Italian. If you struggle to understand some of the clues, you can find them in English in the *Help Section* on page 126

Orizzontali

1. Vengono in mazzi da 52
4. Ha sei facce con i punti
7. Ha tanti pezzi da incastrare
8. Spesso si usa prima della bicicletta
9. Si spinge con un piede solo
11. Vola e ha un lungo filo
12. È rotondo e rotola
13. Amato animale di peluche
14. Con quella Davide ha ucciso Golia

Verticali

2. Dondola avanti e indietro
3. Le più famose sono i Lego
5. Si mettono in fila prima della battaglia
6. Ogni bambina ha la sua preferita
10. Si cerca chi non si vuol far trovare

Il vicino di casa antipatico

Match the Italian words on the left, to the English words on the right.

scorbutico	loud
ficcanaso	aggressive
maleducato	grumbler
dispettoso	rude
invadente	annoying
chiassoso	cranky
fastidioso	indiscreet
aggressivo	gossipy
litigioso	spiteful
brontolone	busybody
indiscreto	argumentative
pettegolo	interfering

Come mostrare amore

Match the Italian words on the left, to the English words on the right.

abbraccio	compliments
carezza	trust
complimenti	caress
ascolto	affection
fiducia	presence
onestà	respect
sostegno	hug
presenza	listening
pazienza	support
tenerezza	patience
affetto	honesty
rispetto	tenderness

Il Battesimo

Below this Word Fit puzzle there is a list of words.
Place the words correctly into the grid.

4 lettere
Nome
Rito

5 lettere
Acqua
Croce

6 lettere
Chiesa

7 lettere
Madrina
Neonato
Padrino

9 lettere
Cristiano
Preghiera
Sacerdote

10 lettere
Sacramento

11 lettere
Benedizione

12 lettere
Celebrazione

L'albero genealogico

Below this Word Fit puzzle there is a list of words.
Place the words correctly into the grid.

5 lettere
Morte

6 lettere
Stirpe

7 lettere
Nascita
Origini
Ricerca

8 lettere
Antenato
Famiglia

9 lettere
Lignaggio
Parentela

10 lettere
Cronologia
Matrimonio

11 lettere
Discendente
Generazione

12 lettere
Consanguineo

34 Quote by Unknown

Replace the numbers in the grid with the correct letters, and reveal the quote.

<u>Hints:</u>   18 = A   11 = B   4 = M   3 = N   10 = O

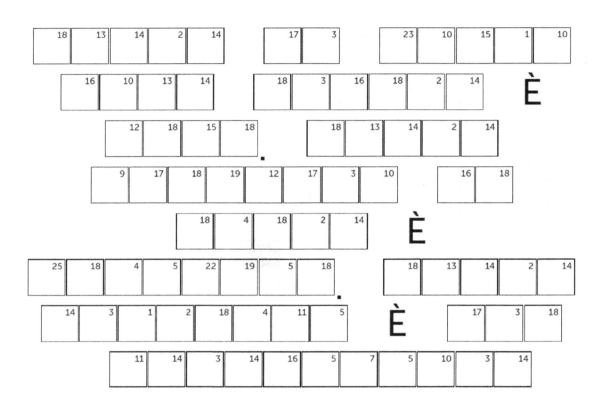

35 Quote by Ralph Waldo Emerson

Replace the numbers in the grid with the correct letters, and reveal the quote.

<u>Hints:</u>   14 = C   22 = E   23 = O   25 = T

Dolce dormire

The following words have been scrambled. Place the letters in the correct order.
For a less challenging version of this puzzle, please turn the page.

IUSCCNO   _ _ _ _ _ _ _

EOLTT   _ _ _ _ _

NSOOG   _ _ _ _ _

POORIS   _ _ _ _ _ _

IILNOPSO   _ _ _ _ _ _ _ _

NOONS   _ _ _ _ _

ILSNOIZE   _ _ _ _ _ _ _ _

ANNANINNNA   _ _ _ _ _ _ _ _ _ _

LLAUC   _ _ _ _ _

TQUEIE   _ _ _ _ _ _

AASUP   _ _ _ _ _

NCLLAIEEPHN   _ _ _ _ _ _ _ _ _ _ _

Dolce dormire

The words on the left have been scrambled. Place the letters in the correct order.

IUSCCNO   C _ _ _ _ _ O

EOLTT   L _ _ _ _

NSOOG   S _ _ _ _

POORIS   R _ _ _ _ O

IILNOPSO   P _ _ _ _ _ _ O

NOONS   S _ _ _ _

ILSNOIZE   S _ _ _ _ _ _ O

ANNANINNNA   N _ _ _ N _ _ _ A

LLAUC   C _ _ _ _

TQUEIE   Q _ _ _ _ E

AASUP   P _ _ _ _

NCLLAIEEPHN   P _ _ _ _ C _ _ _ _ A

Translate the English words below the grid into Italian and find them in the Word Search. If this is too challenging, please turn the page for an easier puzzle.

```
S  N  E  C  S  D  C  J  U  J  S  D  O  Z  C
S  O  R  B  A  L  E  D  N  A  C  J  T  O  U
T  I  P  E  N  O  I  S  I  V  E  L  E  T  S
E  R  J  R  P  V  Y  E  A  I  L  L  P  T  C
R  A  Z  E  A  R  M  A  I  D  E  S  P  E  I
E  D  O  N  I  M  A  V  R  E  D  T  A  N  N
O  A  O  E  F  F  M  S  E  I  N  E  T  I  I
S  P  R  C  A  A  A  O  R  P  A  N  W  M  T
A  M  D  A  R  E  B  A  B  A  C  D  M  A  O
V  A  A  T  G  T  Y  S  I  I  K  E  V  C  D
J  L  U  R  O  N  S  G  L  G  L  O  E  O  I
W  T  Q  O  T  A  G  K  G  G  L  E  I  R  R
E  P  O  P  O  I  G  O  L  O  R  O  V  H  B
F  Y  E  G  F  P  M  L  C  P  J  Y  I  R  I
R  P  O  L  T  R  O  N  A  D  A  P  M  A  L
```

FIREPLACE	BOOKCASE	ORNAMENT
CANDLESTICK	BOOKS	CHAIR
CANDLES	CLOCK	CARPET
CUSHIONS	PLANTS	TABLE
SOFA/COUCH	ARMCHAIR	TELEVISION
PHOTOGRAPH	ASHTRAY	STEREO
LAMP	FOOTREST	CURTAINS
CHANDELIER	PAINTING	VASE

Il soggiorno

Find the Italian words below the grid in the Word Search puzzle. These are the same Italian words as in 37a, but they're located in different positions on the grid.

```
A T D E D I V A N O J N K E L
O E R E T S A I R E R B I L I
S N P I A N T E D N E T D E B
A O R B A L E D N A C Y E D R
V I P I N I C S U C A T I N I
B S E R E N E C A T R O P A L
G I O A A M G M W T A I A C O
Z V L N I M I N A Y D G I X C
D E O O D N M P L Z A O G T I
M L V R E W P O W N P L G X Q
Y E A T S E G P B S M O O V M
R T T L T X O T O I A R P F J
F O T O G R A F I A L O B G P
L A M P A D A R I O H E C I W
H A Y Q R Q U A D R O E P F Y
```

CAMINETTO	LIBRERIA	SOPRAMMOBILE
CANDELABRO	LIBRI	SEDIA
CANDELE	OROLOGIO	TAPPETO
CUSCINI	PIANTE	TAVOLO
DIVANO	POLTRONA	TELEVISIONE
FOTOGRAFIA	PORTACENERE	STEREO
LAMPADA	POGGIAPIEDI	TENDE
LAMPADARIO	QUADRO	VASO

Translate the English words below the grid into Italian and find them in the Word Search. If this is too challenging, please turn the page for an easier puzzle.

```
S  I  J  E  X  K  D  H  O  T  X  T  I  W  R
D  E  R  B  O  T  T  O  L  I  A  G  C  P  O
L  R  T  A  G  R  G  U  O  D  N  Y  Q  F  N
E  B  O  T  S  O  G  A  I  R  A  M  E  E  V
J  M  I  D  E  L  O  C  R  E  M  R  U  I  M
V  E  A  D  I  M  E  G  M  N  I  T  S  D  Z
W  V  R  O  U  M  B  A  A  E  T  O  O  E  G
X  O  B  C  B  U  R  R  G  V  T  M  D  N  N
O  N  B  R  E  Z  E  D  E  S  E  M  I  U  B
I  D  E  V  O  I  G  G  L  N  S  S  N  L  X
A  I  F  M  I  T  I  M  I  D  E  T  R  A  M
N  U  J  H  G  U  A  C  R  T  Y  Y  O  B  F
N  H  C  W  G  V  A  B  P  V  M  D  I  M  Q
E  O  N  N  A  S  H  A  A  O  S  Y  G  I  R
G  Q  O  E  M  Q  K  C  F  S  X  G  F  E  M
```

JANUARY	SEPTEMBER	FRIDAY
FEBRUARY	OCTOBER	SATURDAY
MARCH	NOVEMBER	SUNDAY
APRIL	DECEMBER	YEAR
MAY	MONDAY	HOLIDAYS
JUNE	TUESDAY	DAYS
JULY	WEDNESDAY	MONTH
AUGUST	THURSDAY	WEEK

Il calendario

Find the Italian words below the grid in the Word Search puzzle. These are the same
Italian words as in 38a, but they're located in different positions on the grid.

```
T  V  K  D  D  Q  E  L  I  R  P  A  S  G  J
F  Y  H  D  I  Z  G  K  D  X  R  R  A  K  G
I  H  P  Y  P  I  X  U  E  E  J  N  C  A  V
O  I  L  G  U  L  D  K  N  R  S  O  I  N  M
I  N  M  G  F  O  S  U  U  B  I  Z  N  A  O
G  H  N  R  O  I  D  E  L  O  C  R  E  M  G
G  O  T  A  B  A  S  R  T  T  O  A  M  I  A
A  T  N  I  I  R  G  B  X  T  C  M  O  T  S
M  S  P  D  D  B  E  M  Q  O  E  R  D  T  R
Z  O  K  E  R  B  M  E  V  O  N  M  O  E  E
V  G  E  T  E  E  O  C  T  I  X  W  B  S  I
W  A  K  R  N  F  O  I  A  N  N  E  G  R  R
U  X  K  A  E  V  I  D  E  V  O  I  G  N  E
E  S  E  M  V  F  D  J  C  C  P  T  S  O  F
K  I  Z  S  R  X  Q  M  T  T  C  X  J  Q  T
```

GENNAIO	SETTEMBRE	VENERDI
FEBBRAIO	OTTOBRE	SABATO
MARZO	NOVEMBRE	DOMENICA
APRILE	DICEMBRE	ANNO
MAGGIO	LUNEDI	FERIE
GIUGNO	MARTEDI	GIORNI
LUGLIO	MERCOLEDI	MESE
AGOSTO	GIOVEDI	SETTIMANA

Formaggi

Find the Italian words below the grid in the Word Search puzzle.

```
E  N  O  L  O  V  O  R  P  D  Z  R  O  U  A
K  D  N  N  O  N  I  R  O  C  E  P  E  U  Z
A  O  I  E  T  T  A  L  E  C  L  O  D  C  R
W  N  H  D  A  L  O  Z  N  O  G  R  O  G  O
Q  G  C  B  N  E  N  O  P  R  A  C  S  A  M
C  A  C  I  O  C  A  V  A  L  L  O  A  Z  A
F  M  A  A  I  O  I  G  G  E  L  A  T  N  C
O  L  R  L  G  O  G  A  I  S  A  G  A  E  S
N  E  T  T  A  L  I  D  R  O  I  F  R  C  K
T  T  S  J  T  O  M  K  W  E  K  U  R  S  P
I  S  O  A  S  B  R  C  L  Q  I  T  U  E  N
N  A  L  L  E  R  A  Z  Z  O  M  V  B  R  B
A  C  O  N  I  R  P  A  C  E  S  Q  U  C  M
C  A  C  I  O  T  T  A  T  T  O  C  I  R  Z
F  F  R  O  B  I  O  L  A  N  A  R  G  E  G
```

ASIAGO	FIORDILATTE	PECORINO
BURRATA	FONTINA	PROVOLONE
CACIOCAVALLO	GORGONZOLA	RICOTTA
CACIOTTA	GRANA	ROBIOLA
CAPRINO	GRUVIERA	SCAMORZA
CASTELMAGNO	MASCARPONE	STAGIONATO
CRESCENZA	MOZZARELLA	STRACCHINO
DOLCELATTE	PARMIGIANO	TALEGGIO

Salumi

Find the Italian words below the grid in the Word Search puzzle.

```
B  E  A  L  E  D  R  A  T  S  U  M  U  E  U
S  S  X  V  A  L  L  E  D  A  T  R  O  M  A
G  U  A  N  C  I  A  L  E  N  N  P  N  A  L
P  V  I  G  A  B  E  U  T  G  Z  Y  I  L  L
A  W  C  Y  T  N  N  J  J  U  L  K  H  A  A
N  Z  C  C  A  E  O  L  V  I  O  C  G  S  P
C  U  I  F  S  G  P  I  K  N  N  E  L  R  S
E  Z  S  A  S  M  M  J  H  A  I  P  O  T  U
T  O  L  L  E  T  A  L  U  C  H  S  R  N  G
T  D  A  O  R  C  Z  L  R  C  C  N  T  R  I
A  R  S  A  P  P  O  C  P  I  E  O  S  W  T
Z  A  L  S  P  L  R  Z  U  O  T  V  N  T  V
P  L  E  E  O  R  Q  T  G  X  O  D  Q  I  H
E  V  T  R  S  A  T  T  E  H  C  R  O  P  F
S  A  Z  B  L  O  L  L  O  C  O  P  A  C  R
```

BRESAOLA	LARDO	SALSICCIA
CAPOCOLLO	MORTADELLA	SANGUINACCIO
COPPA	MUSTARDELA	SOPPRESSATA
COTECHINO	PANCETTA	SPALLA
CULATELLO	PORCHETTA	SPECK
FINOCCHIONA	PROSCIUTTO	STROLGHINO
GUANCIALE	SALAME	ZAMPONE

Le belle favole

This freeform crossword has the clues in Italian. If you struggle to understand some of the clues, you can find them in English in the *Help Section* on page 126

Orizzontali

2. Viene avvelenata da una mela
4. Miagola e porta gli stivali
5. Si sente brutto ma diventa bellissimo
7. È il fratello di Gretel
12. Anche se fa paura, Bella se ne innamora
13. Gli cresce il naso quando racconta le bugie
14. È bella e dorme per 100 anni

Verticali

1. Perde la scarpa a mezzanotte
3. Sono tre e costruiscono case
6. Trova una lampada magica
8. Porta sempre una bacchetta magica
9. Divora Cappuccetto Rosso
10. Un pesce a strisce bianche e rosse
11. Viene trasformata in una carrozza

Relazioni di famiglia

This freeform crossword has the clues in Italian. If you struggle to understand some of the clues, you can find them in English in the *Help Section* on page 127

Orizzontali

4. Di solito dà il cognome ai figli
6. Spesso non va d'accordo con la nuora
9. L'uomo che la mamma risposa
11. Sono i genitori dei nonni
12. È il figlio dello zio
14. Quelle di Cenerentola erano cattive

Verticali

1. Lui ha i tuoi stessi genitori
2. La persona che ti mette al mondo
3. Sono nati lo stesso giorno
5. La donna che si sposa
7. Il fratello del marito
8. Sorella di papà o mamma
10. È famosa la sua torta in Italia
13. Il marito della figlia

Cucinare

Match the Italian words on the left, to the Italian words on the right.

friggere	mestolo
infornare	colapasta
bollire	polpette
mescolare	spezie
tritare	pizza
pesare	uova
apparecchiare	acqua
scolare	bilancia
frullare	coltello
insaporire	freezer
impanare	tavola
scongelare	olio

Sveglia!

Match the Italian words on the left, to the Italian words on the right.

sbadiglio	lampada
cereali	armadio
allarme	sonno
lenzuola	rasoio
luce	letto
cielo	sveglia
barba	piedi
doccia	ritardo
pantofole	alba
indumenti	colazione
trucco	asciugamano
fretta	specchio

Il bucato

Below this Word Fit puzzle there is a list of words.
Place the words correctly into the grid.

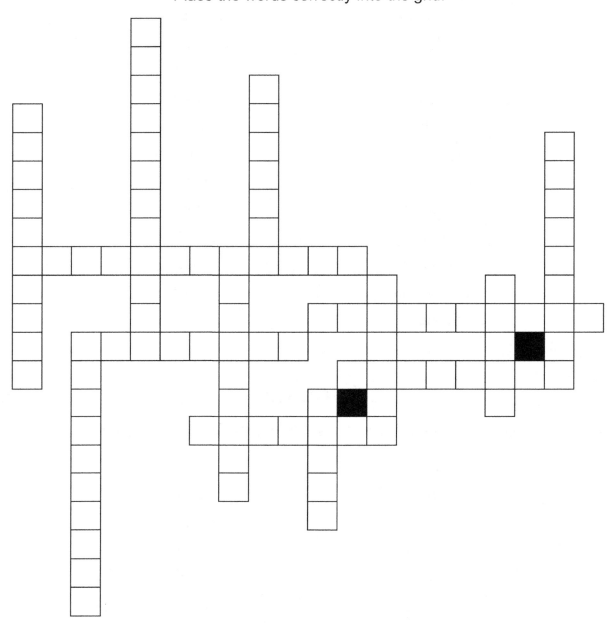

5 lettere
Cesto
Panni

6 lettere
Sapone

7 lettere
Stirare
Piegare

8 lettere
Mollette
Stendere

9 lettere
Detersivo
Lavatrice

10 lettere
Biancheria
Risciacquo
Smacchiare

12 lettere
Ammorbidente
Asciugatrice

Per una serena convivenza

Below this Word Fit puzzle there is a list of words.
Place the words correctly into the grid.

5 lettere	**7 lettere**	**10 lettere**	**12 lettere**
Calma	Dialogo	Equilibrio	Comprensione
Tatto	Perdono	Tolleranza	Condivisione

6 lettere	**8 lettere**	**11 lettere**	
Regole	Pazienza	Concessione	
Valori	Riguardo		
	Rispetto		

47   Quote by Leo Tolstoy

Replace the numbers in the grid with the correct letters, and reveal the quote.

Hints: 12 = A   1 = F   5 = I   17 = O   23 = U

| 9 | 23 | 9 | 9 | 13 | | 6 | 13 |

| 1 | 12 | 11 | 5 | 4 | 6 | 5 | 13 | | 1 | 13 | 6 | 5 | 26 | 5 |

| 7 | 5 | | 7 | 17 | 11 | 5 | 4 | 6 | 5 | 12 | 19 | 17 |,

| 17 | 4 | 19 | 5 | | 1 | 12 | 11 | 5 | 4 | 6 | 5 | 12 |

| 5 | 19 | 1 | 13 | 6 | 5 | 26 | 13 | È

| 5 | 19 | 1 | 13 | 6 | 5 | 26 | 13 | | 12 | | 11 | 17 | 15 | 17 |

| 7 | 23 | 17 |

48   Quote by Benjamin Franklin

Replace the numbers in the grid with the correct letters, and reveal the quote.

Hints: 20 = I   16 = N   5 = O   12 = S

| 17 | 16 | 15 | | 14 | 15 | 12 | 15 | | 16 | 5 | 16 | È

| 17 | 16 | 15 | | 14 | 15 | 12 | 15 | | 12 | 7 | | 16 | 5 | 16 |

| 14 | 5 | 16 | 22 | 20 | 7 | 16 | 7 | | 14 | 20 | 26 | 5 | | 7 |

| 19 | 17 | 5 | 14 | 5 | | 4 | 7 | 9 | | 2 | 15 |

| 8 | 7 | 16 | 22 | 7 | | 7 | | 4 | 7 | 9 | | 20 | 2 |

| 14 | 5 | 9 | 4 | 5 |

54

Cane e gatto

The following words have been scrambled. Place the letters in the correct order.
For a less challenging version of this puzzle, please turn the page.

LROECAL   _ _ _ _ _ _ _

NGILOGAIUZ   _ _ _ _ _ _ _ _ _ _

AFSU   _ _ _ _

ICIOM   _ _ _ _ _

ACINMOAGP   _ _ _ _ _ _ _ _ _

OCDA   _ _ _ _

AMPEZ   _ _ _ _ _

OLPE   _ _ _ _

LOOUICCC   _ _ _ _ _ _ _

IETIVRAOERN   _ _ _ _ _ _ _ _ _ __

EONIFL   _ _ _ _ _ _

IULPC   _ _ _ _ _

Cane e gatto

The words on the left have been scrambled. Place the letters in the correct order.

LROECAL	C _ _ _ _ _ E
NGILOGAIUZ	G _ _ _ Z _ _ _ _ O
AFSU	F _ _ _
ICIOM	M _ _ _ O
ACINMOAGP	C _ _ _ _ G _ _ A
OCDA	C _ _ _
AMPEZ	Z _ _ _ E
OLPE	P _ _ _
LOOUICCC	C _ _ C _ _ _ O
IETIVRAOERN	V _ _ _ R _ _ A _ _ O
EONIFL	F _ _ _ _ O
IULPC	P _ _ _ I

Un litigio in famiglia

Translate the English words below the grid into Italian and find them in the Word Search. If this is too challenging, please turn the page for an easier puzzle.

```
T E R O C N A R B U G I A V W
R O I B B U D F K F T I C Q V
I A C I T I R C R W K T G E J
S E O T T I L F N O C K O E L
T E N O I S N E R P M O C N I
E N C R A O T N A I P G Q O D
Z O I T E K O O T T E P S I D
Z I L N Z C A I B B A R S S S
A S I O L S C Z L C Z C I U T
I S A C A D I A F A O U L L R
S U Z S C P K G L R C D N E I
O C I T S E G E D O C R B D L
L S O T N E M I D A R T I U L
E I N G A Q A P D U G A O M A
G D E R O N O S I D Q N P T E
```

LIE	DOUBT	ANGER
CONFLICT	FEUD	GRUDGE
CRITICISM	JEALOUSY	RECONCILIATION
DISAPPOINTMENT	GESTURES	FIGHT
DISCORD	MISUNDERSTANDING	EXPLANATION
ARGUMENT	TEARS	SCREAMS
SPITE	SWEARWORDS	BETRAYAL
DISHONOUR	CRYING (noun)	SADNESS

Un litigio in famiglia

Find the Italian words below the grid in the Word Search puzzle. These are the same Italian words as in 50a, but they're located in different positions on the grid.

```
F  D  R  A  I  S  O  L  E  G  E  N  T  E  E
G  W  S  E  C  C  A  L  O  R  A  P  T  N  N
O  R  T  N  O  C  S  I  T  S  E  G  O  O  O
S  R  W  O  R  E  R  O  N  O  S  I  D  I  I
T  P  D  I  L  A  Y  V  E  M  Z  I  O  S  S
R  O  M  S  B  I  O  F  M  A  A  K  T  S  N
I  E  R  U  E  D  T  Q  I  B  Z  A  T  U  E
L  Z  G  L  W  R  T  L  D  E  Z  C  E  C  R
L  I  F  E  N  O  I  Z  A  G  E  I  P  S  P
A  O  B  D  W  C  L  F  R  C  T  T  S  I  M
I  T  B  B  N  S  F  B  T  A  S  I  I  D  O
B  N  J  O  M  I  N  Q  D  T  I  R  D  L  C
B  A  C  D  R  D  O  L  Q  D  R  C  N  D  N
A  I  P  E  R  O  C  N  A  R  T  Q  A  D  I
R  P  D  U  B  B  I  O  F  A  I  D  A  U  M
```

BUGIA	DUBBIO	RABBIA
CONFLITTO	FAIDA	RANCORE
CRITICA	GELOSIA	RICONCILIAZIONE
DELUSIONE	GESTI	SCONTRO
DISCORDIA	INCOMPRENSIONE	SPIEGAZIONE
DISCUSSIONE	LACRIME	STRILLA
DISPETTO	PAROLACCE	TRADIMENTO
DISONORE	PIANTO	TRISTEZZA

Erbe e spezie

Translate the English words below the grid into Italian and find them in the Word Search. If this is too challenging, please turn the page for an easier puzzle.

```
R Y H Z T G S D P Y P Q Y M V
E A E E N O I C S E R C T K T
X I B O C I L I S A B Q E O E
K V X T K O L O M E Z Z E R P
A L L E N N A C D A O S S E A
C A U N N I U R R N N F P Z N
I S F A E R W C A A A E X N E
R H N T C A X N G R R I O E S
P Y O U I M H I O O E B R Z F
A G M F N S O Q N I F V O O Y
P A A Z A O N C C G F R L M C
X T S Q H R I C E G A O L I W
W N E A K N M U L A Z L A T X
L E S T O Q U S L M G W G R V
J M C J W J C R O N A G I R O
```

BAY LEAF	TURMERIC	PARSLEY
DILL	TARRAGON	ROSEMARY
ANISEED	MARJORAM	SAGE
BASIL	MINT	MUSTARD
CINNAMON	OREGANO	SESAME
CORIANDER	PAPRIKA	THYME
WATERCRESS	PEPPER	SAFFRON
CUMIN	CHILLI	GINGER

Erbe e spezie

Find the Italian words below the grid in the Word Search puzzle. These are the same Italian words as in 51a, but they're located in different positions on the grid.

```
K  T  N  A  L  I  E  F  W  D  W  R  N  M  I
F  G  I  T  C  D  O  N  A  R  E  F  F  A  Z
K  S  P  N  C  U  I  E  Q  A  I  V  L  A  S
J  P  R  E  P  A  N  E  S  G  G  E  K  Q  E
B  M  V  M  O  N  I  C  N  O  R  E  P  E  P
O  R  O  L  L  A  L  L  E  N  N  A  C  E  M
X  T  Y  K  O  R  I  X  A  C  I  R  P  A  P
R  R  E  U  D  O  L  O  M  E  Z  Z  E  R  P
O  G  H  N  N  I  O  C  I  L  I  S  A  B  E
R  Y  O  N  A  G  I  R  O  L  N  T  M  C  W
E  O  I  J  I  G  H  Z  E  O  E  H  U  S  U
Z  O  N  I  R  A  M  S  O  R  C  M  C  P  F
N  P  M  G  O  M  A  S  E  S  I  W  R  H  H
E  N  O  I  C  S  E  R  C  N  N  S  U  L  W
Z  E  F  A  T  K  R  L  O  C  A  O  C  Y  I
```

ALLORO	CURCUMA	PREZZEMOLO
ANETO	DRAGONCELLO	ROSMARINO
ANICE	MAGGIORANA	SALVIA
BASILICO	MENTA	SENAPE
CANNELLA	ORIGANO	SESAMO
CORIANDOLO	PAPRICA	TIMO
CRESCIONE	PEPE	ZAFFERANO
CUMINO	PEPERONCINO	ZENZERO

La frutta

Translate the English words below the grid into Italian and find them in the Word Search. If this is too challenging, please turn the page for an easier puzzle.

```
G U K Y F M Q A L O G A R F U
Z W W E O M F E N O M I L V E
S K M R I W A I R U G N A E N
I Q A N G U R P B H O A A Q M
H E R A E A I G E I L I C U A
Y U E E D N C M I A L A S C J
Z N P N G A W C N D I P E E H
G Q A O D R U A O W T A P G R
N M I L O G N A M C R P U O A
Q F C E N A T Q L B I H C A C
Q V N M S L C V E F M B R T V
Q A A N U E N O P M A L L P Q
E M R T A M Z E M J D X C A M
E F A N A N A B O C I F L R X
W F X E F I B L P B Z J Z G G
```

APRICOT	STRAWBERRY	BLUEBERRY
PINEAPPLE	RASPBERRY	BLACKBERRY
WATERMELON	LEMON	PAPAYA
ORANGE	MANDARIN	PEAR
BANANA	MANGO	PEACH
PERSIMMON	APPLE	GRAPEFRUIT
CHERRY	POMEGRANATE	PLUM
FIG	MELON	GRAPES

La frutta

Find the Italian words below the grid in the Word Search puzzle. These are the same Italian words as in 52a, but they're located in different positions on the grid.

```
P  P  Q  O  K  Z  L  T  Q  S  M  A  R  O  M
H  S  W  U  G  A  N  A  R  G  A  L  E  M  M
X  G  J  C  M  I  C  T  T  E  N  O  L  E  M
E  Y  P  P  P  G  S  C  N  I  D  G  L  E  B
E  H  O  M  L  E  P  M  O  P  A  A  V  U  I
O  N  K  S  J  I  P  M  L  C  R  R  S  Y  S
E  N  O  M  I  L  F  F  L  N  I  F  B  X  S
H  N  G  C  H  I  C  P  I  B  N  B  R  A  R
O  R  N  A  C  C  E  B  T  A  O  V  L  W  B
Q  P  A  O  A  S  O  S  R  N  Z  J  H  A  K
N  N  M  Q  C  X  K  A  I  R  U  G  N  A  V
B  Y  K  A  N  R  N  N  M  A  F  A  U  B  Y
C  Q  I  X  R  C  W  A  B  J  N  O  Q  V  H
D  Q  Z  B  I  E  N  N  K  A  N  G  U  R  P
X  A  P  A  I  A  P  A  P  M  D  H  F  Q  P
```

ALBICOCCA	FRAGOLA	MIRTILLO
ANANAS	LAMPONE	MORA
ANGURIA	LIMONE	PAPAIA
ARANCIA	MANDARINO	PERA
BANANA	MANGO	PESCA
CACHI	MELA	POMPELMO
CILIEGIA	MELAGRANA	PRUGNA
FICO	MELONE	UVA

Si va in vacanza

This freeform crossword has the clues in Italian. If you struggle to understand some of the clues, you can find them in English in the *Help Section* on page 127

Orizzontali

5. Dove si prende il treno

7. Ospita tende e roulotte

8. Dove si sosta in autostrada

10. Bisogna averla per guidare

11. Si compra prima di viaggiare

12. Viene portato in spalla

13. Alloggio economico

Verticali

1. Una camminata rilassante

2. Dove si affitta la macchina

3. Vacanza sul mare

4. È composto da borse e valigie

6. Casa elegante con giardino

7. Monete e banconote

9. Aiuta a non perdersi

Ora della nanna

This freeform crossword has the clues in Italian. If you struggle to understand some of the clues, you can find them in English in the *Help Section* on page 127

Orizzontali

4. Sta sempre accanto al letto

6. Indumento della notte

9. Saluto prima di andare a dormire

10. Interrompe bruscamente il sonno

12. Si fa quando si dorme

13. Si chiudono la sera e si aprono al mattino

14. Aiuta a far dormire

Verticali

1. Ci appoggi la testa

2. Fa recuperare le energie

3. Tiene caldo durante l'inverno

5. Sono comode da portare ai piedi

7. Viene spenta per addormentarsi

8. La parte morbida del letto

11. Biancheria da letto

Facciamo merenda

The following words have been scrambled. Place the letters in the correct order.
For a less challenging version of this puzzle, please turn the page.

ANPNIO — — — — — —

LEAMTMLAAR — — — — — — — — — —

TUATRF — — — — — —

TEATL — — — — —

OCSCU — — — — —

OSBTTIIC — — — — — — — —

DUINBO — — — — — —

OGYTUR — — — — — —

LRUOFATL — — — — — — — —

ERLECAI — — — — — — —

OTATR — — — — —

KRREACC — — — — — — —

Facciamo merenda

The words on the left have been scrambled. Place the letters in the correct order.

ANPNIO   P _ _ _ _ O

LEAMTMLAAR   M _ _ _ E _ _ _ _ A

TUATRF   F _ _ _ _ A

TEATL   L _ _ _ E

OCSCU   S _ _ _ O

OSBTTIIC   B _ _ C _ _ _ I

DUINBO   B _ _ _ _ O

OGYTUR   Y _ _ _ _ T

LRUOFATL   F _ _ L _ _ _ O

ERLECAI   C _ _ E _ _ I

OTATR   T _ _ _ A

KRREACC   C _ _ C _ _ R

Pasqua

Match the Italian words on the left, to the English words on the right.

uova	Sunday
cioccolato	lamb
pulcino	church
colomba	chocolate
campane	dove
agnello	chick
coniglio	bells
domenica	eggs
risurrezione	rabbit
quaresima	cross
croce	lent
chiesa	resurrection

Facciamo i compiti

Match the Italian words on the left, to the English words on the right.

quaderno	exercise
libro	lesson
matita	study
lezione	revision
ripasso	pencil
ricerca	notebook
studio	book
tema	reading
esercizio	pen
lettura	research
penna	notes
appunti	essay

Articoli di cancelleria

Below this Word Fit puzzle there is a list of words.
Place the words correctly into the grid.

5 lettere	**7 lettere**	**9 lettere**	**12 lettere**
Colla	Forbici	Cucitrice	Calcolatrice
Gomma		Graffette	
Penna	**8 lettere**		**13 lettere**
	Astuccio	**10 lettere**	Evidenziatore
6 lettere	Quaderno	Pennarello	Temperamatite
Matita	Righello		

I rumori di casa

Below this Word Fit puzzle there is a list of words.
Place the words correctly into the grid.

6 lettere	**7 lettere**	**8 lettere**	**10 lettere**
Doccia	Allarme	Friggere	Campanello
Risate	Bussare	Telefono	Starnutire
	Russare		
	Strilla	**9 lettere**	**11 lettere**
	Tossire	Trapanare	Chiacchiere
	Tritare		

60   Quote by George Augustus Moore

Replace the numbers in the grid with the correct letters, and reveal the quote.

Hints: 1 = A   13 = N   11 = O   26 = V

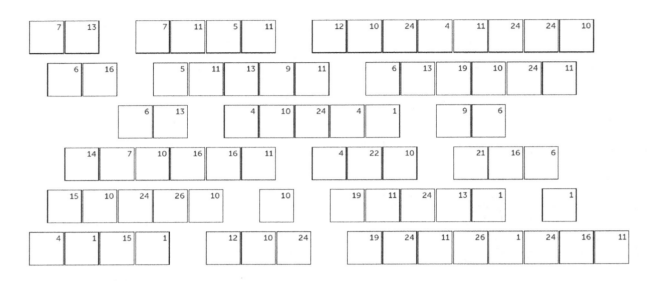

61   Quote by Henry David Thoreau

Replace the numbers in the grid with the correct letters, and reveal the quote.

Hints: 20 = A   9 = E   18 = T   22 = U

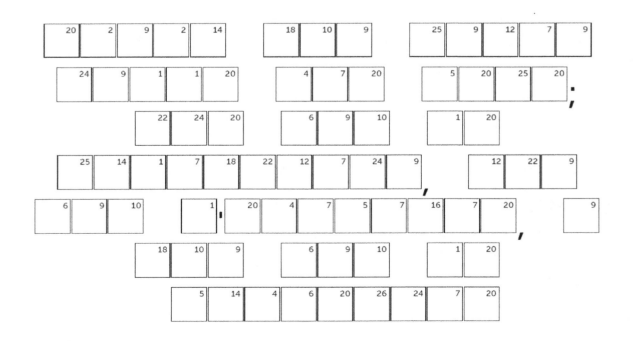

Sul balcone

The following words have been scrambled. Place the letters in the correct order.
For a less challenging version of this puzzle, please turn the page.

IGRHIEANR   _ _ _ _ _ _ _ _ _

ATISV   _ _ _ _ _

EPTNIA   _ _ _ _ _ _

OIIFR   _ _ _ _ _

IALTNOVO   _ _ _ _ _ _ _ _

IESED   _ _ _ _ _

XLRAE   _ _ _ _ _

RIODSA   _ _ _ _ _ _

OSENTIITDO   _ _ _ _ _ _ _ _ _ _

ERISTAGTA   _ _ _ _ _ _ _ _ _

TPCRONERAEE   _ _ _ _ _ _ _ _ _ _ __

OPREATTAP   _ _ _ _ _ _ _ _ _

Sul balcone

The words on the left have been scrambled. Place the letters in the correct order.

IGRHIEANR   R _ _ _ H _ _ _ A

ATISV   V _ _ _ A

EPTNIA   P _ _ _ _ E

OIIFR   F _ _ _ I

IALTNOVO   T _ _ _ L _ _ O

IESED   S _ _ _ E

XLRAE   R _ _ A _

RIODSA   S _ _ _ _ O

OSENTIITDO   S _ _ N _ _ T _ _ O

ERISTAGTA   S _ _ _ R _ _ _ A

TPCRONERAEE   P _ _ T _ _ E _ _ _E

OPREATTAP   P _ _ _ P _ _ _ O

In giardino

Translate the English words below the grid into Italian and find them in the Word Search. If this is too challenging, please turn the page for an easier puzzle.

```
A  O  I  T  A  P  P  J  Q  V  R  J  J  O  A
L  N  B  O  V  O  Y  E  R  A  P  P  A  Z  Z
O  E  N  I  T  A  Z  G  I  L  L  E  C  C  U
U  R  I  A  H  T  E  Y  C  L  M  E  A  P  C
I  R  R  R  F  Y  O  T  T  E  N  I  B  U  R
A  E  E  D  A  F  G  E  H  N  A  W  Y  V  M
Y  T  B  S  E  C  I  R  T  A  I  C  L  A  F
W  C  L  R  R  M  L  A  O  T  A  R  P  O  V
U  D  A  U  A  T  G  T  T  N  K  X  G  G  B
T  M  A  D  N  H  U  N  A  O  H  L  O  R  E
I  E  P  E  I  S  P  A  C  F  I  R  O  I  F
S  A  E  A  M  Q  S  I  C  E  G  O  P  L  J
A  H  I  S  E  A  E  P  E  C  C  A  B  R  E
V  A  Z  A  S  E  C  N  T  A  K  E  H  I  E
Y  S  L  P  R  V  W  H  S  G  E  T  H  G  Q
```

FLOWER-BED	SMALL FOUNTAIN	DECKCHAIR
TREES	GRAVEL	TO SOW
WATERING CAN	PATIO	HEDGE
BUSHES	TO PLANT	FENCE
WEEDS	TO PRUNE/TO TRIM	SOIL
LAWN MOWER	LAWN	BIRDS
FLOWERS	BRANCHES	POTS
LEAVES	TAP	TO DIG/TO HOE

In giardino

Find the Italian words below the grid in the Word Search puzzle. These are the same
Italian words as in 63a, but they're located in different positions on the grid.

```
A O R M F A L O U I A V T B G
W N K F L N B E R A P P A Z H
Z E N B C C S S I L L E C C U
L R E A P T D I A L P Q I N R
X R R R F R O T T E N I B U R
I E A P A F B E A N I L N E Y
R T T I E C I R T A I C L A F
O M O M R M L A O T S B C O A
I N P A A Q G T T N A V G I H
F V H R N H U N A O V L N T K
X C K W I S P A C F I G T A E
C V X A M H S I C E B O E P P
Q V I K E X E P E C C A B R E
B A O D S B C P T P R J S U I
J T J M G E M S S Y P L T H S
```

AIUOLA   FONTANELLA   SDRAIO
ALBERI   GHIAIA   SEMINARE
ANNAFFIATOIO   PATIO   SIEPE
CESPUGLI   PIANTARE   STECCATO
ERBACCE   POTARE   TERRENO
FALCIATRICE   PRATO   UCCELLI
FIORI   RAMI   VASI
FOGLIE   RUBINETTO   ZAPPARE

Utensili e accessori da cucina

Translate the English words below the grid into Italian and find them in the Word Search. If this is too challenging, please turn the page for an easier puzzle.

```
U E U L G G J Q O T U B M I V
I Z C H A I P P A T A V A C A
T B J P A I L G E T E T I I S
O L O T S E M E R G L C G B S
K A N G X V T R O E O B U R O
F I I H O X G O T N T B T O I
E C P O L O T T A R A B T F O
R N M E L I T I L A C V A F N
E A A Y E C C L L C S A R R I
I L T P R C X L U I I L G U L
L I S X A A I O R T R L S S O
G B P I T T T B F T P E B T C
A X H B T E S E P A A D M A N
T C T A A S U O U B B A Z I E
S R X X M A L O T N E P J B T
```

CAN OPENER	BLENDER	SIEVE
JAR/TIN	WHISK	NUTCRACKER
TENDERIZER	GRATER	PASTRY CUTTER
SCALES	FUNNEL	CHOPPING BOARD
KETTLE	ROLLING PIN	BAKING TRAY
WINE OPENER	LADLE	TIMER
STRAINER	FRYING PAN	TOASTER
SCISSORS	SAUCEPAN	TRAY

64b   Utensili e accessori da cucina

Find the Italian words below the grid in the Word Search puzzle. These are the same Italian words as in 64a, but they're located in different positions on the grid.

```
S F R U S T A I O E O I S T I
S C O A I C N A L I B C T I M
A J H B P O N I L O C I A M B
X O D I P B U C E B X B M E U
E L O T A C S I R P A R P R T
R O L T T C D S A T B O I A O
O T O E A Z C A T A X F N L R
T T T G V K T I T P C F O L V
A A S L A D C G A L O T N E P
L R E I C A U U M N X N R D M
L A M A R M C T O I O S S A V
U B E N A P A T S O T C K P D
R J E O I C C A T E S Q I E L
F X D H O P E R O T I L L O B
Q U E R E I L G A T Y N N J T
```

APRISCATOLE	FRULLATORE	SETACCIO
BARATTOLO	FRUSTA	SCHIACCIANOCI
BATTICARNE	GRATTUGIA	STAMPINO
BILANCIA	IMBUTO	TAGLIERE
BOLLITORE	MATTARELLO	TEGLIA
CAVATAPPI	MESTOLO	TIMER
COLINO	PADELLA	TOSTAPANE
FORBICI	PENTOLA	VASSOIO

Oggi Sposi

Translate the English words below the grid into Italian and find them in the Word Search. If this is too challenging, please turn the page for an easier puzzle.

```
H  R  P  V  D  R  K  V  T  S  V  B  A  M  D
S  O  H  S  E  L  L  E  G  I  M  A  D  V  C
Z  V  H  G  C  A  E  Y  D  S  O  U  O  Q  E
L  C  A  B  O  I  N  O  M  I  R  T  A  M  B
Z  L  I  F  R  L  O  T  Y  D  I  C  I  M  A
I  Y  O  T  A  G  M  T  B  N  M  P  N  B  F
D  T  I  D  Z  I  I  E  P  I  A  U  O  J  A
E  U  G  I  I  M  T  H  J  R  A  A  M  D  T
F  O  D  R  O  A  S  C  E  B  Y  T  I  H  S
E  Z  Z  O  N  F  E  N  R  E  A  S  R  B  E
Y  P  E  I  I  J  T  A  N  R  C  U  E  O  F
F  F  J  F  Q  I  Q  B  T  O  I  C  C  U  T
I  N  V  I  T  A  T  I  R  M  S  O  F  Z  M
V  M  J  W  F  M  O  S  I  A  U  L  P  Q  H
E  T  E  U  Q  U  O  B  U  K  M  X  H  I  U
```

DRESS	DECORATIONS	MARRIAGE
FRIENDS	SPEECH	MUSIC
LOVE	FAMILY	WEDDING
BANQUET	WEDDING RINGS	RELATIVES
BOUQUET	JOY	GIFTS
TOAST	PARTY	WITNESS
CEREMONY	FLOWERS	CAKE
BRIDESMAIDS	GUESTS	VOWS

Oggi Sposi

Find the Italian words below the grid in the Word Search puzzle. These are the same Italian words as in 65a, but they're located in different positions on the grid.

```
U  K  G  V  I  R  O  I  F  P  J  E  I  H  N
S  P  L  C  E  Y  T  W  B  F  O  N  S  D  F
L  V  J  G  T  A  I  O  E  A  O  O  I  E  F
B  G  A  C  I  S  U  M  Z  I  I  M  D  V  K
G  L  T  P  H  Q  K  N  Z  L  N  I  N  R  J
I  L  R  E  U  V  A  A  O  G  O  T  I  B  A
O  N  O  E  T  G  R  I  N  I  M  S  R  Z  T
S  L  T  L  F  O  N  M  T  M  I  E  B  B  S
R  G  V  L  C  Z  L  S  H  A  R  T  I  B  E
O  T  T  E  H  C  N  A  B  F  T  K  T  Y  F
C  Q  D  G  O  D  L  E  D  M  A  I  O  I  G
S  A  D  I  T  N  E  R  A  P  M  R  V  L  C
I  C  I  M  A  N  T  O  J  H  K  H  Q  N  M
D  A  W  A  I  N  O  M  I  R  E  C  Z  N  I
T  T  D  D  K  Q  W  A  S  F  P  Y  N  O  H
```

ABITO	DECORAZIONI	MATRIMONIO
AMICI	DISCORSO	MUSICA
AMORE	FAMIGLIA	NOZZE
BANCHETTO	FEDI	PARENTI
BOUQUET	GIOIA	REGALI
BRINDISI	FESTA	TESTIMONE
CERIMONIA	FIORI	TORTA
DAMIGELLE	INVITATI	VOTI

Un bel libro

This freeform crossword has the clues in Italian. If you struggle to understand some of the clues, you can find them in English in the *Help Section* on page 128

Orizzontali

4. Genere poliziesco
6. Il genere perfetto per i romantici
8. Il personaggio più importante
9. Vi si prendono in prestito i libri
11. Si scrive in versi
12. Può essere di diversi generi
13. Appare sempre sulla copertina

Verticali

1. La storia di una persona
2. Le parti del libro
3. Le scrivono i critici e lettori
5. Ti ricorda cos'hai letto per ultimo
7. Chi scrive il libro
8. Il libro lungo ne ha tante
10. Storia fantastica per bambini

La festa di San Valentino

This freeform crossword has the clues in Italian. If you struggle to understand some of the clues, you can find them in English in the *Help Section* on page 128

Orizzontale

2. Gesti di tenerezza e affetto

5. Due persone che stanno insieme

7. Si offrono in un mazzo

8. Si dà con le labbra

10. L'angelo arciere

11. Si prova per l'amato

12. Fa piacere darlo e riceverlo

13. Sentimentale e idealista

Verticale

1. Quello fondente ha più cacao

3. Dove descrivi i tuoi sentimenti

4. Stravedono l'uno per l'altra

6. Il mese in cui si festeggia

9. Il simbolo dell'amore

13. Il colore della passione

Abbigliamento e parti del corpo

Match the Italian words on the left, to the Italian words on the right.

guanti	collo
calzini	orecchie
pantaloni	dito
reggiseno	polso
sciarpa	testa
cappello	piedi
anello	viso
trucco	gambe
bracciale	seno
orecchini	spalle
cintura	mani
scialle	vita

Dolci e delizie

Match the Italian words on the left, to the Italian words on the right.

panettone	rum
tiramisù	frutta
amaretti	vin santo
gelato	mandorle
crostata	latte
meringa	cioccolato
cannolo	mascarpone
babà	ricotta
brownie	marmellata
pasticcini	uvetta
macedonia	albumi
cantucci	crema

Carnevale

Find the Italian words below the grid in the Word Search puzzle.

```
A Q E T A S I R A E E O C E D
E S T S T E N O L A T N A P F
T L F Z T L H F L N Z I N P A
A I R G E L L A E I R H I A J
L A B A B E P M N L H C B R D
I L O A M T I R I L B C M F F
F L F T O T L G C A Z E O U I
S E G S R I O W L B E L L I I
R H S E T R D A U E Z R O C G
N G V F M F N A P Z P A C L T
Y I N O I Z A R O C E D Q O B
D R G I O O I A R B B E F D K
X B D N D E R E H C S A M U L
M Q E N W Y O I G G E R A I V
I N O Z N A C C O S T U M I L
```

ALLEGRIA	COSTUMI	GIOCHI
ARLECCHINO	DECORAZIONI	MASCHERE
BALANZONE	DIVERTIMENTO	PANTALONE
BALLI	DOLCI	PULCINELLA
BRIGHELLA	FEBBRAIO	RISATE
CANZONI	FESTA	SFILATE
COLOMBINA	FRAPPE	TROMBETTA
CORIANDOLI	FRITTELLE	VIAREGGIO

Alcune materie di scuola

The following words have been scrambled. Place the letters in the correct order.
For a less challenging version of this puzzle, please turn the page.

TALIONAI   _ _ _ _ _ _ _ _

TOSARI   _ _ _ _ _ _

CSAFEREN   _ _ _ _ _ _ _ _

FIREAGOGA   _ _ _ _ _ _ _ _ _

IMAMACTEAT   _ _ _ _ _ _ _ _ _ _

IITDTOR   _ _ _ _ _ _ _

MAIICHC   _ _ _ _ _ _ _

SOOFIIAFL   _ _ _ _ _ _ _ _ _

ICIFSA   _ _ _ _ _ _

GEESLIN   _ _ _ _ _ _ _

OLGIEEINR   _ _ _ _ _ _ _ _ _

OILIGAOB   _ _ _ _ _ _ _ _

Alcune materie di scuola

The words on the left have been scrambled. Place the letters in the correct order.

TALIONAI   I _ _ L _ _ _ O

TOSARI   S _ _ _ _ A

CSAFEREN   F _ _ N _ _ _ E

FIREAGOGA   G _ _ _ R _ _ _ A

IMAMACTEAT   M _ _ E _ _ T _ _ A

IITDTOR   D _ _ I _ _ O

MAIICHC   C _ _ M _ _ A

SOOFIIAFL   F _ _ _ S _ _ _ A

ICIFSA   F _ _ _ _ A

GEESLIN   I _ _ L _ _ E

OLGIEEINR   R _ _ _ G _ _ _ E

OILIGAOB   B _ _ L _ _ _ A

Le carni

Translate the English words below the grid into Italian and find them in the Word Search. If this is too challenging, please turn the page for an easier puzzle.

```
G U Q P V E C I N R E P T I A
B N X H E A I C S O C F M P C
Z W F P V T O N A I G A F O N
T B Q A O S T O S C I U N G A
G O L L T N S O S V B I X Q I
J L T O A E C K O G G J U Q B
O L L T G W A T R L J A I B X
L E E T E E L A I H G N I C B
L N E E F R O O S L A S N V B
E G G L P A P P I R T B N I E
T A L I V P P A P E L A I A M
I M X F O N I H C C A T N R W
V K W L I E N C T M P S Z S I
Q Y L H P N A R T A N A F Y S
U O Z N A M U H H R C B X U G
```

LAMB	THIGH	PARTRIDGE
DUCK	RIBS	CHICKEN
WHITE	PHEASANT	QUAIL
STEAK	LIVER	RED
KID	FILLET	ESCALOPE
HORSE	PORK	TURKEY
WILD BOAR	BEEF	TRIPE
RABBIT	BREAST	VEAL

Le carni

Find the Italian words below the grid in the Word Search puzzle. These are the same
Italian words as in 72a, but they're located in different positions on the grid.

```
V  L  T  F  M  E  O  L  L  A  V  A  C  S  Y
U  X  T  E  S  C  G  O  N  A  I  G  A  F  L
O  V  Z  F  R  M  H  I  D  Y  D  O  I  K  M
L  O  A  X  A  P  P  I  R  T  E  P  M  D  G
V  L  N  N  I  P  O  S  O  L  L  E  N  G  A
J  L  Z  E  O  I  L  G  I  N  O  C  G  I  C
U  O  F  L  T  N  O  L  L  E  T  I  V  K  N
C  P  A  A  T  R  I  P  A  B  S  N  I  Z  A
A  C  I  I  E  O  O  H  I  I  O  R  Y  O  I
S  H  L  H  R  V  T  S  C  B  C  E  Y  W  B
S  I  G  G  P  M  T  I  S  C  W  P  V  P  P
O  F  A  N  A  E  E  Y  O  T  A  G  E  F  A
R  P  U  I  C  A  L  M  C  A  R  T  A  N  A
K  M  Q  C  H  A  I  V  D  Y  T  D  F  S  X
E  L  A  I  A  M  F  D  B  O  I  H  O  O  Y
```

AGNELLO	COSCIA	PERNICE
BIANCA	COSTOLE	POLLO
BIANCA	FAGIANO	QUAGLIA
BISTECCA	FEGATO	ROSSA
CAPRETTO	FILETTO	SCALOPPINA
CAVALLO	MAIALE	TACCHINO
CINGHIALE	MANZO	TRIPPA
CONIGLIO	PETTO	VITELLO

Translate the English words below the grid into Italian and find them in the Word Search. If this is too challenging, please turn the page for an easier puzzle.

```
E  A  T  O  R  T  E  L  O  G  N  O  V  P  D
N  N  Q  I  U  M  H  J  L  B  X  U  K  U  B
I  G  O  P  X  E  C  O  Y  O  A  X  S  G  C
G  U  N  M  M  A  I  O  P  L  O  P  T  N  J
G  I  N  A  L  N  R  Z  A  N  I  D  R  A  S
U  L  O  C  R  A  T  Z  F  G  P  V  A  A  D
M  L  T  S  M  T  S  U  O  I  V  H  G  J  C
A  A  R  A  X  S  O  L  L  E  S  A  N  Q  R
A  T  L  L  P  O  A  R  Y  O  M  P  I  J  D
Q  A  B  O  V  G  I  E  B  B  M  C  R  C  L
C  R  O  I  D  A  L  M  E  M  C  X  A  H  D
V  O  T  L  W  R  G  R  Z  O  O  H  Y  H  L
G  Q  V  G  O  A  I  H  Z  R  R  G  H  O  C
W  B  D  O  D  F  R  X  O  Q  J  D  S  T  A
X  G  D  S  G  C  T  J  C  U  U  X  D  H  A
```

EEL	MULLET	SCAMPI
LOBSTER	HAKE	MACKEREL
HERRING	SEA BREAM	SOLE
SQUID	OYSTERS	SEA BASS
CARP	OCTOPUS	TUNA
MUSSELS	TURBOT	RED MULLET
PRAWNS	SALMON	TROUT
COD	SARDINE	CLAMS

Il pesce

Find the Italian words below the grid in the Word Search puzzle. These are the same Italian words as in 73a, but they're located in different positions on the grid.

```
A  N  G  U  I  L  L  A  N  I  D  R  A  S  T
L  O  U  F  Q  D  W  B  A  P  R  A  C  R  P
O  L  L  E  S  A  N  A  A  M  V  A  O  W  G
I  F  P  L  E  N  O  M  L  A  S  T  S  C  Z
L  J  Q  O  F  E  Z  Z  O  C  A  S  T  Z  G
G  G  A  G  B  A  Q  Y  Z  S  X  O  R  H  O
O  G  G  N  E  N  I  G  G  U  M  G  I  L  N
S  P  R  O  B  O  R  A  M  A  L  A  C  R  O
H  S  L  V  Z  R  E  L  J  I  Q  R  H  O  U
H  Z  G  O  O  B  B  O  J  L  A  A  E  B  R
S  D  D  N  P  M  M  G  H  G  O  G  F  M  P
D  G  C  N  S  O  A  I  T  I  M  N  P  O  Q
V  S  X  O  B  G  G  P  I  R  V  I  J  R  N
Z  X  P  T  G  S  U  S  A  T  A  R  O  B  J
J  O  G  W  O  C  H  F  D  W  C  A  K  B  P
```

ANGUILLA	MUGGINE	SCAMPI
ARAGOSTA	NASELLO	SGOMBRO
ARINGA	ORATA	SOGLIOLA
CALAMARO	OSTRICHE	SPIGOLA
CARPA	POLPO	TONNO
COZZE	ROMBO	TRIGLIA
GAMBERI	SALMONE	TROTA
MERLUZZO	SARDINA	VONGOLE

Giochiamo a carte

Find the Italian words below the grid in the Word Search puzzle.

```
O  L  O  C  A  N  N  I  P  Q  E  E  T  N  C
I  R  O  U  C  O  H  B  I  X  R  R  E  O  D
R  E  K  O  P  D  U  D  A  K  Z  A  N  Z  E
A  U  A  E  T  T  E  S  S  E  R  T  F  Z  N
T  A  B  R  K  D  S  I  R  T  A  R  V  A  O
I  P  V  A  L  O  C  S  I  R  B  A  R  M  P
L  O  N  I  M  A  R  L  E  E  K  C  W  I  O
O  C  J  H  Y  A  L  A  C  S  Z  S  N  R  C
S  S  D  C  P  R  Z  K  B  P  A  E  M  O  S
B  V  W  S  V  E  P  Z  N  D  L  N  B  I  E
M  M  Q  I  U  I  V  Y  E  L  U  P  K  F  H
U  J  C  M  B  M  J  N  A  T  S  A  N  A  C
W  F  Y  Z  R  I  A  B  O  S  T  T  O  K  C
N  Z  J  O  H  R  G  H  Y  L  L  O  J  D  I
K  R  Y  G  I  P  O  D  B  I  A  A  G  F  P
```

ASSO	MAZZO	RUBAMAZZETTO
BRISCOLA	MISCHIARE	SCALA
CANASTA	PICCHE	SCARTARE
CONTARE	PINELLA	SCOPA
CUORI	PINNACOLO	SCOPONE
DENARI	POKER	SOLITARIO
FIORI	PRIMIERA	TRESSETTE
JOLLY	RAMINO	TRIS

Quando non stiamo bene

This freeform crossword has the clues in Italian. If you struggle to understand some of the clues, you can find them in English in the *Help Section* on page 128

Orizzontali

2. Ti fa sempre starnutire
4. Quando si perdono i sensi
6. Misura la temperatura
10. Una casa per i malati
11. Rottura di un osso
12. Può farti perdere l'equilibrio
13. Visita il paziente
14. Può causare il mal di denti

Verticali

1. Protegge una piccola ferita
3. Si chiama in caso di emergenza
5. Un sintomo della bronchite
7. Un fortissimo mal di testa
8. Alta temperatura
9. Dove compri le medicine

Il primo giorno di scuola (elementare)

This freeform crossword has the clues in Italian. If you struggle to understand some of the clues, you can find them in English in the *Help Section* on page 129

Orizzontali

4. La borsa che contiene tutto
6. Si fa prima della lezione
8. Suona quando è ora di entrare
10. Il banco dell'insegnante
11. La pausa molto importante
13. La stanza dove si impara
14. Si prova salutando la mamma

Verticali

1. Si indossa per andare a scuola
2. Viene occupato dall'allievo
3. Amico di classe
5. La donna che insegna
7. L'insegnante ci scrive col gesso
9. Tiene le penne e matite
12. Frequentano la scuola

77

Sotto il letto del bambino

Match the Italian words on the left, to the English words on the right.

mostro	tissue
calzino	drawing
briciole	sock
gatto	waste paper
giocattolo	crumbs
ragno	cat
ciabatta	toy
adesivo	comic book
disegno	slipper
fazzoletto	monster
giornalino	spider
cartacce	sticker

78

Prendiamoci il tè

Match the Italian words on the left, to the English words on the right.

teiera	milk
zucchero	brew
biscotti	teapot
torta	cup
tazza	lemon
piattino	napkins
cucchiaino	biscuits
infuso	tray
latte	saucer
limone	cake
tovaglioli	sugar
vassoio	teaspoon

Parti di un capo d'abbigliamento

Below this Word Fit puzzle there is a list of words.
Place the words correctly into the grid.

4 lettere
Orlo

5 lettere
Asola
Tasca

6 lettere
Manica

7 lettere
Bottoni
Corpino
Polsino
Ripresa

8 lettere
Cerniera
Colletto
Elastico

9 lettere
Cappuccio
Etichetta

10 lettere
Scollatura

La festa di Capodanno

This freeform crossword has the clues in Italian. If you struggle to understand some of the clues, you can find them in English in the *Help Section* on page 129

Orizzontali

1. Più sono, meglio è
3. Fondamentale per ballare
7. L'ultimo mese dell'anno
9. Si fa dicendo *cin cin*
11. Il banchetto di fine anno
13. Un vino con le bollicine
14. Sempre buoni per il futuro

Verticali

2. Saluto finale
4. Decorano la sala
5. Chiude l'anno vecchio
6. Si prende bevendo troppo
8. Rimangono nella memoria
10. Esplosioni dei petardi
12. L'opposto di vecchio

Legumi e frutta secca

The following words have been scrambled. Place the letters in the correct order.
For a less challenging version of this puzzle, please turn the page.

IECLTHNICE   _ _ _ _ _ _ _ _ _ _

GAOIIFL   _ _ _ _ _ _ _

ECIC   _ _ _ _

AFVE   _ _ _ _

IEPLLIS   _ _ _ _ _ _ _

ICRDIAHA   _ _ _ _ _ _ _ _

CDARNAAI   _ _ _ _ _ _ _ _

AEGTCASN   _ _ _ _ _ _ _ _

ONPILI   _ _ _ _ _ _

HSICICPAT   _ _ _ _ _ _ _ _ _

OLICCEON   _ _ _ _ _ _ _ _

ANELDROM   _ _ _ _ _ _ _ _

Legumi e frutta secca

The words on the left have been scrambled. Place the letters in the correct order.

IECLTHNICE   L _ _ T _ _ C _ _ E

GAOIIFL   F _ _ I _ _ I

ECIC   C _ _ _

AFVE   F _ _ _

IEPLLIS   P _ _ _ _ _ I

ICRDIAHA   A _ _ C _ _ _ I

CDARNAAI   A _ _ C _ _ _ I

AEGTCASN   C _ _ T _ _ _ E

ONPILI   P _ _ _ _ I

HSICICPAT   P _ _ _ A _ _ _ I

OLICCEON   N _ _ C _ _ _ E

ANELDROM   M _ _ D _ _ _ E

Le verdure

Translate the English words below the grid into Italian and find them in the Word Search. If this is too challenging, please turn the page for an easier puzzle.

```
C G B D S E D A N O G O R J O
W A N I H C C U Z G R G L N C
P N V Y E R X C A G U T T A L
L A P O N I L O I G A F V L E
K Z Z I L L E S I P Z O L O W
B N Y H X F M X U C L R T T Y
F A I C M W I O L O I R T E C
L L N C Y V D O A L L O P I C
H E I O G N U F R L W P S B R
H M C N Y E N O R E P E P U O
T B A I R O C I C N R A C R W
S H N F P F N C N A T O R A C
X I I E I R L R P V L W Z Z I
K G P Z B O G A R A P S A G P
V R S O L O C C O R B P D T A
```

ASPARAGUS	CHICORY	PEPPER
CHARD	ONION	LEEK
BROCCOLI	GREEN BEAN	TURNIP
ARTICHOKE	MUSHROOM	RADISH
CARROT	FENNEL	ROCKET
CAULIFLOWER	LETTUCE	CELERY
CABBAGE	AUBERGINE	SPINACH
CUCUMBER	PEAS	COURGETTE

Le verdure

Find the Italian words below the grid in the Word Search puzzle. These are the same Italian words as in 82a, but they're located in different positions on the grid.

```
A  L  O  T  E  I  B  G  D  D  W  P  A  C  T
P  G  G  A  N  I  H  C  C  U  Z  G  G  O  X
A  C  A  O  O  L  O  C  C  O  R  B  U  L  U
R  A  A  O  R  N  E  D  B  M  F  F  T  O  C
Y  I  L  L  E  S  I  P  E  A  I  U  T  I  Q
O  R  L  O  P  O  L  L  E  N  A  V  A  R  H
I  O  O  V  E  K  A  L  O  C  U  R  L  T  D
O  C  P  A  P  N  I  C  F  I  O  F  K  E  R
K  I  I  C  Z  F  C  K  O  T  G  F  C  C  C
W  C  C  A  V  H  A  V  I  I  A  A  C  O  Q
C  X  N  T  I  B  N  T  C  W  R  H  F  I  R
C  A  V  O  L  F  I  O  R  E  A  F  I  M  H
H  U  O  R  R  O  P  J  A  D  P  S  A  M  L
P  O  N  A  D  E  S  J  C  K  S  L  X  Z  C
F  D  F  C  F  U  N  G  O  M  A  N  A  R  G
```

ASPARAGO	CICORIA	PEPERONE
BIETOLA	CIPOLLA	PORRO
BROCCOLO	FAGIOLINO	RAPA
CARCIOFO	FUNGO	RAVANELLO
CAROTA	FINOCCHIO	RUCOLA
CAVOLFIORE	LATTUGA	SEDANO
CAVOLO	MELANZANA	SPINACI
CETRIOLO	PISELLI	ZUCCHINA

Attività del tempo libero

Translate the English words below the grid into Italian and find them in the Word Search. If this is too challenging, please turn the page for an easier puzzle.

```
U M V A A T A C I P M A R R A
N A O M S I N O I S R U C S E
C R I O M S I L C I C H H I N
I U G F C G Y L T H V P Y T O
N T G T A E O E O C U O N X I
E T A T R R F Z T C G G G C Z
T I N M U A G I E A Z N A D A
T R I J T R M O T C Q N O W T
O C D O T O U N T S T K T P I
N S R H E L C I E O J S I K D
G B A P L O S S C I F T C K E
E X I U R C W M C P T M U C M
S Y G S Y K E O E U G Z C D T
I C A L C I O E R A N I C U C
D R I C A M O A F I D S P U U
```

CLIMBING	SEWING	MEDITATION
SOCCER	DANCING	SWIMMING
SINGING	DRAWING	PAINTING
CYCLING	HIKING	EMBROIDERY
COLLECTING	PHOTOGRAPHY	CHESS
COLOURING	DARTS	WRITING
JOGGING	GARDENING	CROCHET
COOKING	READING	YOGA

Attività del tempo libero

Find the Italian words below the grid in the Word Search puzzle. These are the same Italian words as in 83a, but they're located in different positions on the grid.

```
O  I  G  G  A  N  I  D  R  A  I  G  Q  C  C
M  G  Q  U  E  T  T  E  C  C  E  R  F  O  E
S  F  V  D  I  Z  A  R  U  T  T  I  R  C  S
I  I  C  S  T  I  H  C  C  A  C  S  D  A  D
N  O  M  A  C  I  R  I  I  T  A  O  A  C  I
O  T  T  E  N  I  C  N  U  P  V  Q  I  D  S
I  I  F  M  K  L  F  H  E  A  M  W  F  T  E
S  C  J  O  I  C  L  A  C  G  C  A  A  H  G
R  U  R  S  E  E  O  O  T  O  U  N  R  A  N
U  C  M  C  G  K  N  L  L  Y  N  R  G  R  O
C  O  L  L  E  Z  I  O  N  I  S  M  O  U  A
S  T  I  T  U  A  R  U  T  T  I  P  T  T  Z
E  N  O  I  Z  A  T  I  D  E  M  Y  O  T  N
R  A  Z  Z  R  Z  H  C  P  A  Z  B  F  E  A
D  C  J  E  R  A  N  I  C  U  C  Z  X  L  D
```

ARRAMPICATA	CUCITO	MEDITAZIONE
CALCIO	DANZA	NUOTO
CANTO	DISEGNO	PITTURA
CICLISMO	ESCURSIONISMO	RICAMO
COLLEZIONISMO	FOTOGRAFIA	SCACCHI
COLORARE	FRECCETTE	SCRITTURA
CORSA	GIARDINAGGIO	UNCINETTO
CUCINARE	LETTURA	YOGA

Translate the English words below the grid into Italian and find them in the Word Search. If this is too challenging, please turn the page for an easier puzzle.

```
R  B  G  Q  D  K  A  I  L  G  A  V  O  T  A
K  O  K  H  C  A  R  E  I  T  T  U  R  F  P
E  T  A  S  O  P  O  L  L  E  T  L  O  C  P
B  T  K  A  L  O  T  O  I  C  E  L  A  S  A
U  I  V  F  O  O  M  N  C  I  H  B  P  A  R
R  G  Z  F  I  F  I  I  A  U  C  A  A  R  E
R  L  U  A  L  O  V  A  T  O  R  T  N  E  C
I  I  P  R  G  O  S  I  I  E  O  P  Z  I  C
E  A  P  A  A  T  J  H  C  H  F  N  W  R  H
R  N  I  C  V  T  X  C  E  D  C  Q  U  E  I
A  I  E  F  O  A  H  C  P  U  K  C  T  H  A
M  Z  R  Q  T  I  H  U  E  L  Q  J  U  C  R
X  Z  A  P  A  P  I  C  P  O  S  T  O  C  E
Y  A  A  R  E  I  T  A  L  A  S  N  I  U  T
P  T  E  R  E  I  H  C  C  I  B  I  H  Z  V
```

TO SET THE TABLE	TEASPOON	SEAT
GLASS	SPOON	SALT
BOTTLE	FORK	TO CLEAR THE TABLE
BUTTER DISH	FRUIT BOWL	SMALL CUP
JUG	SALAD BOWL	TABLECLOTH
CENTREPIECE	PEPPER	NAPKIN
BOWL	PLATE	SUGAR BOWL
KNIFE	CUTLERY	SOUP TUREEN

A tavola

Find the Italian words below the grid in the Word Search puzzle. These are the same
Italian words as in 84a, but they're located in different positions on the grid.

```
A  R  E  I  T  A  L  A  S  N  I  S  L  U  O
L  P  R  H  E  R  V  O  L  L  E  T  L  O  C
O  E  P  E  P  E  E  I  A  F  F  A  R  A  C
V  N  O  A  E  I  L  A  A  L  O  T  O  I  C
A  E  L  D  R  R  A  I  L  G  I  T  T  O  B
T  A  O  K  A  E  S  H  I  F  S  E  T  I  T
O  N  I  A  I  H  C  C  U  C  T  H  C  P  O
R  I  L  R  H  C  J  C  O  G  Y  C  B  O  V
T  Z  G  E  C  C  I  U  H  M  H  R  A  S  A
N  Z  A  I  C  U  M  C  K  I  W  O  H  A  G
E  A  V  T  E  Z  X  P  E  C  A  F  V  T  L
C  T  O  T  R  Z  O  R  B  B  T  R  E  E  I
M  X  T  U  A  R  E  I  R  R  U  B  E  U  A
J  V  F  R  P  Z  U  P  P  I  E  R  A  F  C
J  F  K  F  S  P  I  A  T  T  O  T  S  O  P
```

APPARECCHIARE	CUCCHIAINO	POSTO
BICCHIERE	CUCCHIAIO	SALE
BOTTIGLIA	FORCHETTA	SPARECCHIARE
BURRIERA	FRUTTIERA	TAZZINA
CARAFFA	INSALATIERA	TOVAGLIA
CENTROTAVOLA	PEPE	TOVAGLIOLO
CIOTOLA	PIATTO	ZUCCHERIERA
COLTELLO	POSATE	ZUPPIERA

The following words have been scrambled. Place the letters in the correct order.
For a less challenging version of this puzzle, please turn the page.

VIAINRSAC _ _ _ _ _ _ _ _ _

IEDSA _ _ _ _ _

UTCEOMRP _ _ _ _ _ _ _ _

NTAPATESM _ _ _ _ _ _ _ _ _

LNTFOEOE _ _ _ _ _ _ _ _

AERTISAT _ _ _ _ _ _ _ _

MRCHSOE _ _ _ _ _ _ _

LEACARTL _ _ _ _ _ _ _ _

ISTRAETSCEA _ _ _ _ _ _ _ _ _ __

AOCREIDALN _ _ _ _ _ _ _ _ _ _

HBCECAA _ _ _ _ _ _ _

RLLENAIEACC _ _ _ _ _ _ _ _ _ __

L'ufficio in casa

The words on the left have been scrambled. Place the letters in the correct order.

VIAINRSAC   S _ _ _ V _ _ _ A

IEDSA   S _ _ _ A

UTCEOMRP   C _ _ _ U _ _ _

NTAPATESM   S _ _ _ P _ _ _ E

LNTFOEOE   T _ _ _ F _ _ O

AERTISAT   T _ _ _ I _ _ A

MRCHSOE   S _ _ _ _ _ O

LEACARTL   C _ _ T _ _ _ A

ISTRAETSCEA   C _ _ S _ _ T _ _ _ A

AOCREIDALN   C _ _ E _ _ A _ _ O

HBCECAA   B _ _ _ _ _ A

RLLENAIEACC   C _ _ C _ _ L _ _ _ A

I mostri

Match the Italian words on the left, to the Italian words on the right.

dracula	pozione
ciclope	serpenti
minotauro	inferi
licantropo	extraterrestre
zombie	toro
mummia	vampiro
strega	gigante
fantasma	fuoco
medusa	spirito
drago	cimitero
alieno	lupo
cerbero	bende

I versi degli animali (dentro e fuori casa)

Match the Italian words on the left, to the Italian words on the right.

cane	gracchia
corvo	miagola
gallo	ronza
gatto	tuba
grillo	squittisce
passero	gracida
piccione	frinisce
rana	stride
topo	canta
zanzara	cinguetta
pipistrello	gufa
gufo	abbaia

Tipi di pasta

Find the Italian words below the grid in the Word Search puzzle.

```
X V A Z I N I N A D E S M P R
I N I T A C U B I L L I S U F
N T E N N E P E L L A F R A F
I I T H I L L E C I M R E V E
L T T M N L T L G I M U Q I N
A T E E O A L L L A H M A C I
T E N I I T T E L L E P P A C
I H I L L L R D T H I D L P C
D G G G G A A R W R N E I I U
C A E I I S V A F N O T N P T
T P R H T A I P Y Y T T G E T
Y S B C R G O P J L A E U T E
T E Q N O N L A G T G V I T F
S O C O T E I P R Y I A N E R
U I H C C O N G P B R B E Q S
```

BAVETTE	GNOCCHI	RIGATONI
BUCATINI	LASAGNE	SEDANINI
CAPPELLETTI	LINGUINE	SPAGHETTI
CONCHIGLIE	PAPPARDELLE	TAGLIATELLE
DITALINI	PENNE	TORTELLINI
FARFALLE	PIPETTE	TORTIGLIONI
FETTUCCINE	RAVIOLI	VERMICELLI
FUSILLI	REGINETTE	ZITI

Translate the English words below the grid into Italian and find them in the Word Search. If this is too challenging, please turn the page for an easier puzzle.

```
T Y W E Y O F R Z L Q P D I S
A N N O G E T U S U B B W N Y
I L I W L O T I T S E V A I H
C N L P E T T A B A I C C C N
I L A V I T S J V A O K C N U
M D D Q Y O V A B R E S A O W
A I N I M P E R M E A B I L E
C S A N R P S E N O I L G A M
E T S I N A G I D R A C L T Q
P D E Z Y C O T I D A R F N I
R H N L M Y A T T E I L G A M
A Q R A I I N O L A T N A P X
C K L C T K O N E S I G G E R
S N A E J U I A T T A V A R C
U D D P Q N M C Y F X T A Q I
```

SUIT	SWEATSHIRT	PANTS/KNICKERS
SOCKS	JACKET	SHORTS
SHIRT/BLOUSE	SKIRT	TROUSERS
VEST	RAINCOAT	BRA
COAT	FLIP FLOPS	SANDALS
CARDIGAN	JEANS	SHOES
SLIPPERS	T-SHIRT	BOOTS
TIE	JUMPER	DRESS

Abbigliamento

Find the Italian words below the grid in the Word Search puzzle. These are the same Italian words as in 89a, but they're located in different positions on the grid.

```
A I C I M A C C A V A S K G J
N N A N D J W A I R I N E D J
N I L A D N A S E D N A T U M
O Z E N O I L G A M I E S B X
G L C N A F G G W W C J C Z C
O A T T E I L G A M N L E V Y
T C R L S U F S P L O W T E C
I M P E R M E A B I L E T P D
D A N T I Y N A T T A V A R C
A O O T I T S E V O T I B A E
R S T R A D T I D D N E A C R
F V L L O T T O P P A C I S N
N Q O P A P E O N D P J C X B
I N A G I D R A C A C C A I G
I L A V I T S H K C C U P S H
```

ABITO	FELPA	MUTANDE
CALZINI	GIACCA	PANTALONCINI
CAMICIA	GONNA	PANTALONI
CANOTTIERA	IMPERMEABILE	REGGISENO
CAPPOTTO	INFRADITO	SANDALI
CARDIGAN	JEANS	SCARPE
CIABATTE	MAGLIETTA	STIVALI
CRAVATTA	MAGLIONE	VESTITO

Accessori e gioielli

Translate the English words below the grid into Italian and find them in the Word Search. If this is too challenging, please turn the page for an easier puzzle.

```
R  C  J  O  O  T  T  E  L  O  Z  Z  A  F  O
U  O  Q  I  L  A  I  H  C  C  O  T  L  M  L
K  L  S  G  A  N  E  L  L  O  T  G  B  A  L
O  L  T  O  I  L  G  O  F  A  T  R  O  P  E
L  A  X  L  Z  N  V  V  V  N  E  E  N  R  P
O  N  Q  O  J  G  I  A  X  L  I  L  I  A  P
D  A  S  R  O  B  R  H  L  F  H  L  L  I  A
N  F  P  O  A  C  V  O  C  V  C  E  L  C  C
O  I  L  G  A  T  N  E  V  C  R  T  E  S  S
I  F  H  M  O  E  H  F  N  J  E  E  S  S  C
C  A  R  U  T  N  I  C  C  W  C  R  R  P  I
K  E  L  A  I  C  C  A  R  B  L  B  O  I  A
F  M  A  N  T  E  L  L  A  W  I  S  B  L  L
G  E  M  E  L  L  I  T  N  A  U  G  J  L  L
N  Y  S  G  V  G  T  P  L  V  W  V  K  A  E
```

RING	PENDANT	UMBRELLA
BAG/HANDBAG	NECKLACE	EARRINGS
PURSE	HANDKERCHIEF	WATCH
BRACELET	TIE PIN	WALLET
BRACES	CUFFLINKS	SCARF
HAT	GLOVES	SHAWL
HAIRBAND	CAPE	BROOCH
BELT	GLASSES	FAN

Accessori e gioielli

Find the Italian words below the grid in the Word Search puzzle. These are the same
Italian words as in 90a, but they're located in different positions on the grid.

```
R E T K O T T E L O Z Z A F O
M C G O I G O L O R O T X M V
U X O L L E P P A C T A B B L
E I L O I L G O F A T R O P N
L O L D S A D D V L E U N K U
L H E N L I F A A L I T I A M
A I N O N C R X L E H N L P O
I L A I H C C O L T C I L R I
C L S C A A B J I N R C E A L
S E X M J R O G P A E C S I G
L M R R D B M J S M C B R C A
G E L L E T E R B H S S O S T
F G B O R S A F I H F Q B B N
O Q Y A V V A N A L L O C K E
K T N Y Y F I T N A U G O W V
```

ANELLO
BORSA
BORSELLINO
BRACCIALE
BRETELLE
CAPPELLO
CERCHIETTO
CINTURA

CIONDOLO
COLLANA
FAZZOLETTO
FERMACRAVATTA
GEMELLI
GUANTI
MANTELLA
OCCHIALI

OMBRELLO
ORECCHINI
OROLOGIO
PORTAFOGLIO
SCIARPA
SCIALLE
SPILLA
VENTAGLIO

Relax serale

This freeform crossword has the clues in Italian. If you struggle to understand some of the clues, you can find them in English in the *Help Section* on page 129

Orizzontali

4. Un tempo era solo in bianco e nero
6. Scambio di idee ed opinioni
7. Tengono i piedi caldi
10. Fa felici le orecchie
11. Lo accarezzi e fa le fusa
12. Un tè alle erbe
13. Assenza di rumori

Verticali

1. Si porta sopra il pigiama
2. Un quaderno personale
3. Sedile per più persone
5. Contemplazione nella quiete
7. Sedia soffice e comoda
8. Si fa tenendo un libro
9. Sono imbottiti e confortevoli

Il trasloco

This freeform crossword has the clues in Italian. If you struggle to understand some of the clues, you can find them in English in the *Help Section* on page 130

Orizzontali

4. Utile per andar su e giù
6. Necessarie per entrare a casa
7. Di solito sono di cartone
9. La lista completa di tutto
10. Lo sono il gas, l'elettricità e l'acqua
12. Ne hai uno nuovo quando cambi casa
13. Si fanno togliendo lo sporco
14. Il prestito per acquistare la casa

Verticali

1. Si può rompere facilmente
2. Si smontano e si rimontano
3. Serve per trasportare tutto
5. È adesivo e si usa per imballare
8. Indicano il contenuto
11. Si arrotola e si lega

Una brava babysitter

The following words have been scrambled. Place the letters in the correct order.
For a less challenging version of this puzzle, please turn the page.

TLENAPUU   _ _ _ _ _ _ _ _

FTEASUFTAO   _ _ _ _ _ _ _ _ _

ACIIPSTMA   _ _ _ _ _ _ _ _

EVDRTEENIT   _ _ _ _ _ _ _ _ _

USARPROEM   _ _ _ _ _ _ _ _

TETTAAN   _ _ _ _ _ _ _

FAFLABIEDI   _ _ _ _ _ _ _ _ _

AZEEPTNI   _ _ _ _ _ _ _

OPMIRCNEVAS   _ _ _ _ _ _ _ _ _ __

AAPCCE   _ _ _ _ _ _

TLAIBADTEA   _ _ _ _ _ _ _ _ _

SOAETN   _ _ _ _ _ _

Una brava babysitter

The words on the left have been scrambled. Place the letters in the correct order.

TLENAPUU	P _ _ T _ _ _ E
FTEASUFTAO	A _ _ _ T _ _ _ _ A
ACIIPSTMA	S _ _ _ A _ _ _ A
EVDRTEENIT	D _ _ _ R _ _ _ _ E
USARPROEM	P _ _ _ U _ _ _ A
TETTAAN	A _ _ _ _ _ A
FAFLABIEDI	A _ _ _ D _ _ _ _ E
AZEEPTNI	P _ _ _ E _ _ E
OPMIRCNEVAS	C _ _ P _ _ N _ _ _ A
AAPCCE	C _ _ _ _ E
TLAIBADTEA	A _ _ _ T _ _ _ _ E
SOAETN	O _ _ _ _ A

Facciamo le pulizie

Translate the English words below the grid into Italian and find them in the Word Search. If this is too challenging, please turn the page for an easier puzzle.

```
P O L V E R E E T M A E E E L
F B C K E R A N I F O R T S A
A R E N E I G I C O E A N Z V
P L R N J X S D A V R R A B A
A O O I N P O R L I A E T H R
R I M Z U E Z O E S U V T H E
E C O G Z R P S T R Q L E L E
I C N U B A A I A E C O F U F
M A N A R N P D N T A P N C S
U R A I Q I O S G E I S I E E
T T P H K D C X A D C V S N C
T S W C I R S V R G S G I T C
A N O C R O P S Z N I Z D E H
P E R A D I C U L Z R O A Y I
L O Z M A R U T A Z Z A P S O
```

VACUUM CLEANER	STAIN	BUCKET
DETERGENT	CLOTH	BRUSH
DISINFECTANT	DUSTBIN	RUBBISH/TRASH
MESS	DUST	TO DUST
HYGIENE	COBWEB	DIRTY
TO WASH	TO TIDY UP	SPONGE
TO POLISH	TO RINSE	RAG
SHINY	BROOM	TO SCRUB

Facciamo le pulizie

Find the Italian words below the grid in the Word Search puzzle. These are the same
Italian words as in 94a, but they're located in different positions on the grid.

```
S P A Z Z O L A D E N E I G I
E R G L T O V I S R E T E D S
O I H C C E S G D A N E E A L
O O W L Y O H R L R J R T S U
B E O C R O P S X E E A N T C
E R A D I C U L G V R U A R E
C A I H C C A M L L A Q T A N
W N C Y S V Z O W O N C T C T
E I T M A O P V N P I A E C E
H F S R F A P O C S D I F I S
N O E E R E V L O P R C N O P
A R E I M U T T A P O S I N U
D T P K V B V Q N A I I S N G
P S A L E T A N G A R R I A N
A R U T A Z Z A P S E A D P A
```

ASPIRAPOLVERE   MACCHIA   SECCHIO
DETERSIVO   PANNO   SPAZZOLA
DISINFETTANTE   PATTUMIERA   SPAZZATURA
DISORDINE   POLVERE   SPOLVERARE
IGIENE   RAGNATELA   SPORCO
LAVARE   RIORDINARE   SPUGNA
LUCIDARE   RISCIACQUARE   STRACCIO
LUCENTE   SCOPA   STROFINARE

Qualità di un bravo genitore

Translate the English words below the grid into Italian and find them in the Word Search. If this is too challenging, please turn the page for an easier puzzle.

```
O O S O R U M E R P O E E I P
N A T S I M I T T O V L L Q R
E G E O T A C U D E I I I B U
R E L I T N E G M B S B B D D
E L R R B I E O A T N A I L E
S A E O N O T S P B E D N E N
E N T B S S N O W O R I O M T
N O N A A O E U C P F P P E
S I A L P I T T T I M F S A S
I Z R S O G R T N T O A I T I
B A E U N G E E E A C O D I N
I R L M E A V F I P E A O C C
L H L I S R I F Z M S S M O E
E C O L T O D A A I W I B I R
H C T E O C N X P S D I R M O
```

AFFECTIONATE	KIND/NICE	RESPONSIBLE
RELIABLE	HARD-WORKING	RESPECTFUL
UNDERSTANDING	HONEST	SENSITIVE
BRAVE	OPTIMIST	SERENE
AVAILABLE	PATIENT	LIKEABLE
FUNNY	CARING	SINCERE
POLITE	PRUDENT	TOLERANT
EMPATHETIC	RATIONAL	HUMBLE

Qualità di un bravo genitore

Find the Italian words below the grid in the Word Search puzzle. These are the same Italian words as in 95a, but they're located in different positions on the grid.

```
R O N E S T O E H D D E I F E
X E T N E T R E V I D T Y E M
I O S O T T E P S I R N W N P
Z T Z P Q G U P Y X T A R O A
O A L E O S O I G G A R O C T
S C A L V N O O N E R E S I I
O U T I I E S X G T B L O T C
R D S B S L O A Y N R L U A O
U E I A N I I U B E H O T P R
M L M D E B R M C I X T T M E
E I I I R I O I W Z L R E I C
R T T F P S B L V A G E F S N
P N T F M N A E C P Y K F N I
X E O A O E L A N O I Z A R S
P G T E C S P R U D E N T E Z
```

AFFETTUOSO	GENTILE	RESPONSABILE
AFFIDABILE	LABORIOSO	RISPETTOSO
COMPRENSIVO	ONESTO	SENSIBILE
CORAGGIOSO	OTTIMISTA	SERENO
DISPONIBILE	PAZIENTE	SIMPATICO
DIVERTENTE	PREMUROSO	SINCERO
EDUCATO	PRUDENTE	TOLLERANTE
EMPATICO	RAZIONALE	UMILE

Tipi di dolci

Find the Italian words below the grid in the Word Search puzzle.

```
F R I T T E L L E A I A I G C
O I W Z L Y J O T A L E G R A
M Q E I L G O F E L L I M N S
E E N O R R O T E E E H R C S
M H O G Y O T T E N R O C I A
T O L O N N A C W O T M F A T
I D O I N I C C I T S A P B A
T D B Z L C X I T T E R A M A
T E M G Z N T S K E N T P O T
O R O T T O I U D N A I G L A
C F B S R N T L J A C W I O T
S I I T Y N N I Q P H E K C S
I M A E L A P O R O D N A P O
B E O I C C U T N A C S R B R
S S J I N A L L E B M A I C C
```

AMARETTI
BISCOTTI
BOMBOLONE
CANESTRELLI
CANNOLO
CANNONCINO
CANTUCCIO
CASSATA

CIAMBELLA
CORNETTO
COLOMBA
CROSTATA
FRITTELLE
GELATO
GIANDUIOTTO
MARITOZZO

MILLEFOGLIE
PANDORO
PANETTONE
PASTICCINI
SEMIFREDDO
SFOGLIATELLA
TORRONE
TORTA

Passatempi

This freeform crossword has the clues in Italian. If you struggle to understand some of the clues, you can find them in English in the *Help Section* on page 130

Orizzontali

3. Il collezionare francobolli
7. Si fa con carta e penna o la tastiera
8. La passione del preparare i cibi
11. Per gli uccelli è naturale
13. L'attività di risolvere cruciverba e rebus
14. L'arte di immortalare un'istante

Verticali

1. Cura del prato e delle piante
2. Esiste ad olio o ad acquerello
4. Disegno su un tessuto con ago e filo
5. Gioco di strategia con re e regina
6. Si fa intrecciando la lana coi ferri
9. Si mischiano prima di giocare
10. Si può fare di un libro, rivista o giornale
12. Il muoversi al suon di musica

Facciamoci belli

This freeform crossword has the clues in Italian. If you struggle to understand some of the clues, you can find them in English in the *Help Section* on page 130

Orizzontali

5. Si applica sulle unghie
6. Cura delle mani e delle unghie
8. Rende i capelli morbidi
10. Chi è calvo non lo usa
12. Lava i denti con lo spazzolino
13. Mette in evidenza le ciglia
14. Meglio calda che fredda

Verticali

1. Fragranza gradevole
2. Maschera il cattivo odore
3. Colora le labbra
4. Fa sempre la schiuma
7. Fondamentale per farsi la barba
9. Riflette la nostra immagine
11. Idrata la pelle

Una cena con amici

Below this Word Fit puzzle there is a list of words.
Place the words correctly into the grid.

5 lettere
Festa
Relax

6 lettere
Invito
Ospiti
Tavola

7 lettere
Battute

8 lettere
Allegria
Appetito
Baldoria
Brindisi

9 lettere
Banchetto
Compagnia

11 lettere
Manicaretti

13 lettere
Conversazione

Un funerale in famiglia

Below this Word Fit puzzle there is a list of words.
Place the words correctly into the grid.

4 lettere
Bara

5 lettere
Addio
Morte
Tomba

6 lettere
Chiesa
Lapide
Pianto

8 lettere
Cimitero

9 lettere
Preghiera
Sepoltura

10 lettere
Commozione
Crematorio

11 lettere
Processione

12 lettere
Condoglianze

Freeform Crosswords – Clues in English

4 – Un neonato in casa

Across

2. A chair with a tray
3. Tender and loving gestures
7. She gives parents a break
11. Where the baby sleeps
12. Where the baby gets changed
13. The baby's feeding bottle
14. A new mum is often deprived of it

Down

1. They hurt the baby's tummy
4. It can comfort the baby
5. It takes the baby for a stroll
6. They wake up the parents
8. A soft toy
9. It needs to be changed often
10. It gets tied around the baby's neck

5 – Facciamo colazione

Across

4. You can find it natural or with fruit
7. It makes a funny noise when coffee is ready
8. It tastes better when in season
10. Coffee with frothy milk
12. Spreadable fruit
13. You use it to wipe your lips
14. They are sweet and come in various shapes

Down

1. It's white and gets drunk at any age
2. It has less calories than sugar
3. Used to mix the sugar in the cup
5. It's produced by bees
6. You drink tea from it
9. The most popular one is filled with custard
11. Served in a bowl with milk

16 – Spaghetti al pomodoro

Across

4. It's shorter if you like them al dente
5. It has to boil for a few minutes
6. Where you serve the pasta
8. You grate it on the plate
10. It gives the sauce a lovely aroma
11. If it's missing, they are insipid

Down

1. Utensil with many holes
2. You roll them on the fork
3. They taste better when fresh
5. It's fried lightly for a stronger flavour
6. It's needed to cook the pasta
7. The best comes from olives
9. It's used to mix the pasta and the sauce

17 – Bricolage/Fai da te

Across

3. It grabs nuts and bolts
4. It has steps and it's portable
6. It's perfect to cut wood
8. It lets you take the correct measurements
10. You hit it with the hammer
11. It's used to make holes
12. It shows if a surface is horizontal

Down

1. You turn it to tighten the screw
2. It covers and protects the furniture
4. It's useful when applying filler
5. It's used to apply paint
7. It lets you turn nuts and bolts
9. Portable lamp
10. It joins and sticks things together

21 – Una passeggiata in centro

Across

3. They protect you from the sun and the rain
5. The *Trevi* one is famous
8. It gets heavy at rush hour
9. They are usual at the end of season
11. Where you go shopping
12. The place you stop for a coffee
13. It's packed with stalls

Down

1. It gets busy on a hot day
2. You need it to buy things
3. It's perfect for taking a break
4. Where pedestrians walk
6. Where the merchandise is put on show
7. It can carry many passengers
10. It's often adorned with a monument

28 – Facciamo una torta

Across

2. One is not enough
6. They break easily
7. Instructions to be followed
8. It makes the cake rise
10. It helps to mix the ingredients
11. It melts easily
13. You light them on a birthday

Down

1. It makes the cake sweet
3. Metal tray where you pour the mixture
4. The quantity of an ingredient
5. White powder
9. Container where you prepare the mixture
10. It must always be hot
12. It's usually whipped

29 – Giochi e giocattoli

Across

1. They come in packs of 52
4. It has six sides with dots
7. A picture of many interlocking pieces
8. It's used before the first bicycle
9. You push it along with one foot
11. It flies and has a long string
12. It's round and it rolls
13. Beloved soft animal toy
14. David used it to kill Goliath

Down

2. It swings back and forth
3. The most popular are called Lego
5. You lined them up before the battle
6. Every little girl has a favourite one
10. You look for who doesn't want to be found

41 – Le belle favole

Across

2. She gets poisoned by an apple
4. It miaows and wears boots
5. It feels ugly but becomes beautiful
7. He is Gretel's brother
12. Even though he's scary, Belle falls in love with him
13. His nose grows when he lies
14. She's beautiful and sleeps for 100 years

Down

1. She loses a slipper at midnight
3. It's three of them and they like to build houses
6. He finds a magic lamp
8. She always carries a magic wand
9. It devours Little Red Riding Hood
10. A fish with orange and white stripes
11. It gets turned into a carriage

42 – Relazioni di famiglia

Across

4. Usually children take his surname
6. She often doesn't get on with the daughter-in-law
9. The new guy that Mum marries
11. They're the parents of grandparents
12. The son of my uncle
14. Cinderella's were mean and unkind

Down

1. You share your parents with him
2. She gave birth to you
3. They are born on the same day
5. The woman you marry
7. Your husband's brother
8. The sister of Mum or Dad
10. Her cake is popular in Italy
13. Your daughter's husband

53 – Si va in vacanza

Across

5. Where you catch your train
7. It hosts caravans and tents
8. Where you take a break on a motorway
10. You must have it in order to drive
11. You purchase it before travel
12. You carry it on your back
13. Low cost accommodation

Down

1. A relaxing walk
2. Where you rent a car
3. Holiday on the sea
4. It's made up of bags and suitcases
6. Elegant house with a garden
7. Coins and banknotes
9. It helps you not to get lost

54 – Ora della nanna

Across

4. It's always by your bedside
6. Garment for the night
9. You say it before going to bed
10. It can suddenly interrupt your sleep
12. You can have it when you sleep
13. You close them in the evening and open them in the morning
14. It helps to fall asleep

Down

1. You rest your head on it
2. It allows you to recover your energies
3. It keeps you warm in winter
5. They're comfortable on your feet
7. You switch it off to go to sleep
8. The soft part of the bed
11. Type of bed linen

66 – Un bel libro

Across

4. Detective fiction
6. Perfect genre if you're a romantic
8. The most important character
9. The place where you borrow books
11. It's written in verses
12. It can be of different genres
13. It's always present on the cover

Down

1. A person's life story
2. The sections of a book
3. They're written by readers and critics
5. It reminds you what you were reading last
7. The person who writes the book
8. A thick book has got many
10. A fantastic story for children

67 – La festa di San Valentino

Across

2. Gestures of tenderness and affection
5. Two people who are together
7. They are offered in a bunch
8. Touch with the lips
10. The archer angel
11. You feel it for your beloved
12. It's a pleasure to give and to receive
13. Sentimental and idealistic

Down

1. The plain one contains more cocoa
3. Where you describe your feelings
4. They dote on each other
6. The month it's celebrated
9. The symbol of love
13. The colour of passion

75 – Quando non stiamo bene

Across

2. It always makes you sneeze
4. Temporary loss of consciousness
6. It measures body temperature
10. House for the sick
11. A broken bone
12. It can make you lose your balance
13. He examines the patient
14. It can cause a toothache

Down

1. It protects a small wound
3. You call it in an emergency
5. One of the symptoms of bronchitis
7. A very strong headache
8. High temperature
9. Where you get your medication

76 – Il primo giorno di scuola (elementare)

Across

4. The bag where you put everything
6. It gets done before the lesson
8. It rings when it's time to go in
10. The teacher's desk
11. A very important break
13. The room where pupils learn
14. You feel it when you say goodbye to Mummy

Down

1. You wear it to go to school
2. Where the pupil sits at
3. A classroom friend
5. The class tutor (female)
7. The teacher writes on it with chalk
9. It contains pens and pencils
12. They attend school

80 – La festa di Capodanno

Across

1. The more, the merrier
3. It's necessary if you want to dance
7. The last month of the year
9. You say *cin cin* when you do it
11. New Year's Eve banquet
13. A sparkling wine
14. They are always good for the future

Down

2. The final goodbye
4. They decorate the room
5. When you say goodbye to the old year
6. You get it when you drink too much
8. They stay with you over time
10. Bangs from petards
12. The opposite of old

91 – Relax serale

Across

4. It used to be only in black and white
6. Exchange of ideas and opinions
7. They keep your feet warm
10. It pleases your ears
11. It purrs when you stroke it
12. A herbal tea
13. The absence of noise

Down

1. You wear it over your pyjamas
2. A personal notebook
3. A seat for more than one person
5. Quiet contemplation
7. Soft and comfortable chair
8. You do it holding a book
9. They are padded and cosy

92 – Il trasloco

Across

4. Useful when going up and down
6. They're necessary to get in the house
7. They're usually made of cardboard
9. The complete list of everything
10. Services such as gas, electricity and water
12. You get a new one when you move
13. They are done to get rid of dirt
14. The loan for a home buyer

Down

1. Easily broken
2. They get dismantled and assembled again
3. It's used to transport everything
5. It's sticky and is used when packing
8. They mark what's inside the boxes
11. You roll it and tie it

97 – Passatempi

Across

3. Stamp collecting
7. It can be done on a keyboard or with pen and paper
8. The passion of preparing food
11. It comes naturally to birds
13. Solving crosswords and puzzles
14. The art of creating durable images

Down

1. Growing and caring of plants
2. It can be in oil or watercolour
4. Decoration on fabric with needle and thread
5. Strategic game with King and Queen
6. Interlacing of yarn using needles
9. You shuffle them before playing
10. It can be done with a book or newspaper
12. Moving to the sound of music

98 – Facciamoci belli

Across

5. It is applied to fingernails
6. Care of hands and nails
8. It makes your hair soft
10. The bald man doesn't need one
12. It cleans your teeth with the toothbrush
13. It emphasises your eyelashes
14. It's better hot than cold

Down

1. Pleasant fragrance
2. It masks bad odours
3. It colours your lips
4. It produces a lather or foam
7. It's needed to shave
9. It reflects our image
11. Skin moisturiser

Word Search Solutions

1a – La famiglia

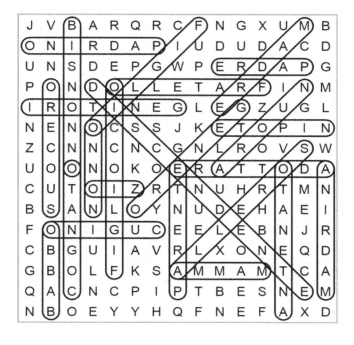

1b – La famiglia

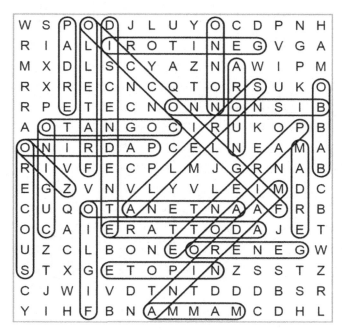

2a – Salutarsi

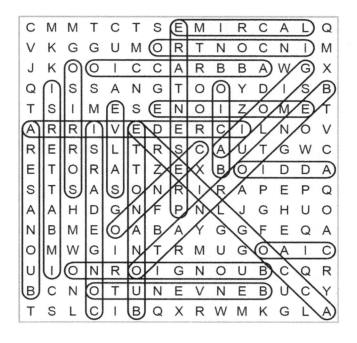

2b – Salutarsi

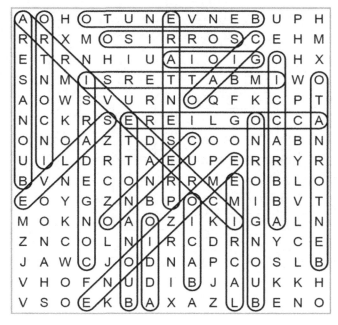

3a – La festa di compleanno

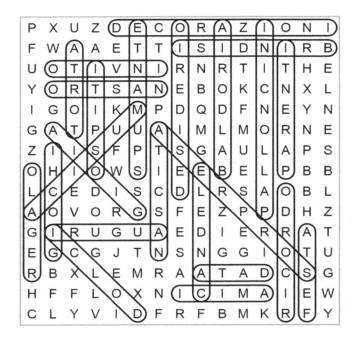

3b – La festa di compleanno

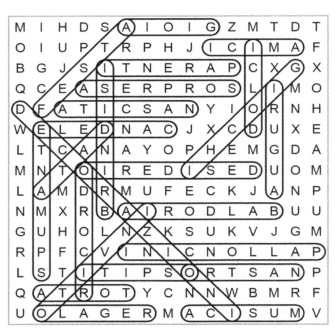

13a – Al supermercato

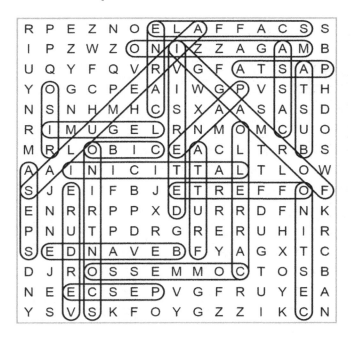

13b – Al supermercato

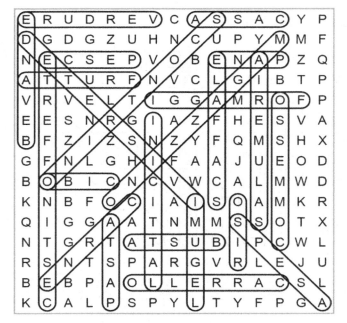

14a – Natale

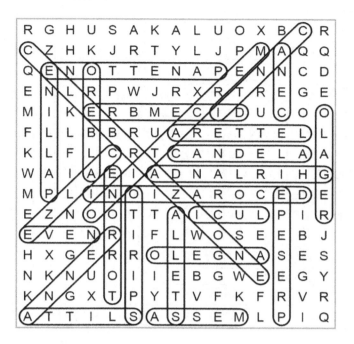

14b – Natale

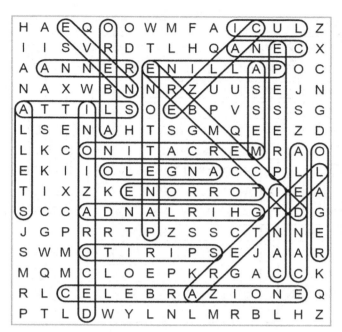

15a – La casa

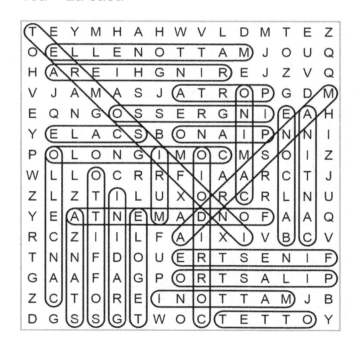

15b – La casa

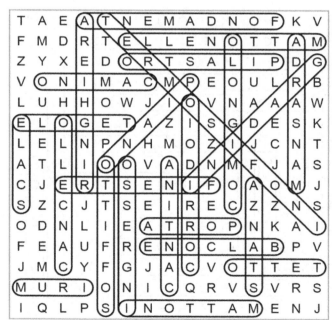

25a – La cucina

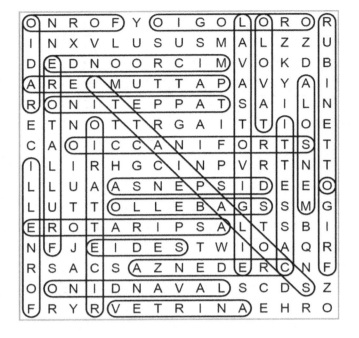

25b – La cucina

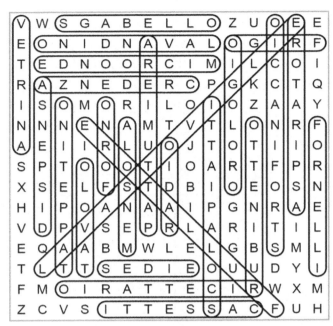

26a – Il bagno

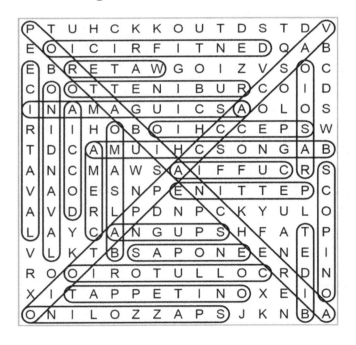

26b – Il bagno

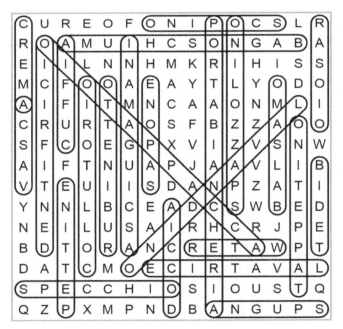

27a – La camera da letto

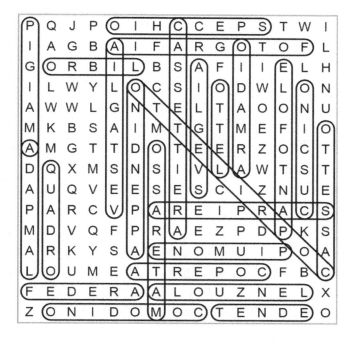

27b – La camera da letto

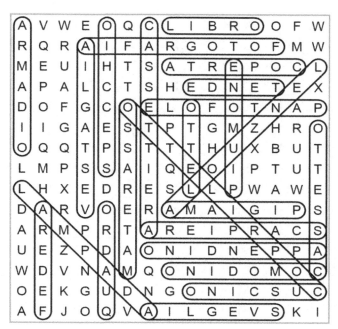

37a – Il soggiorno

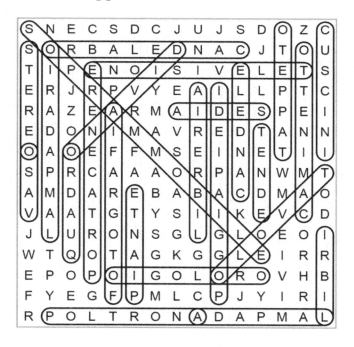

37b – Il soggiorno

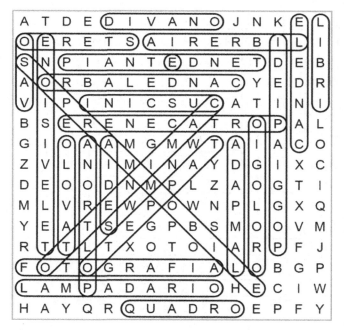

38a – Il calendario

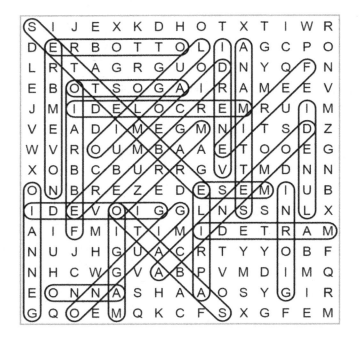

38b – Il calendario

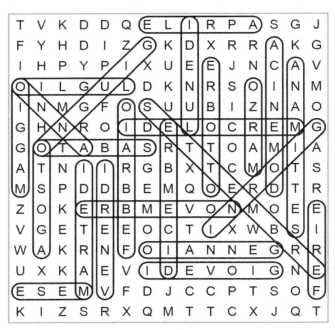

39 – Formaggi

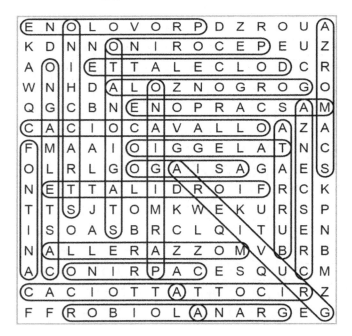

40 – Salumi

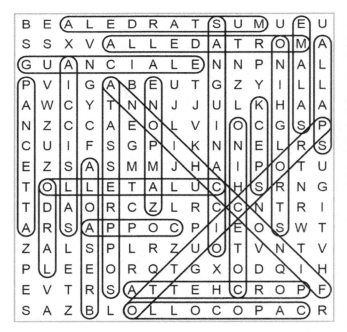

50a – Un litigio in famiglia

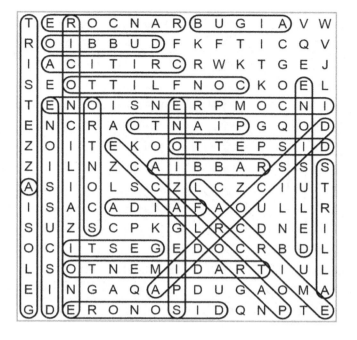

50b – Un litigio in famiglia

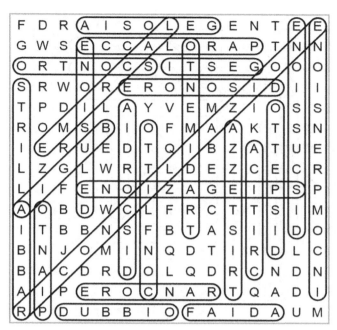

51a – Erbe e spezie

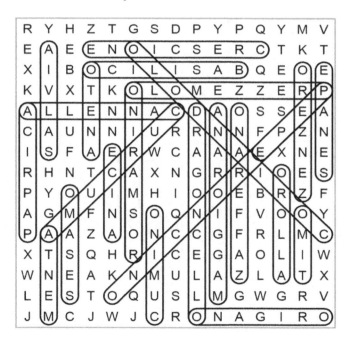

51b – Erbe e spezie

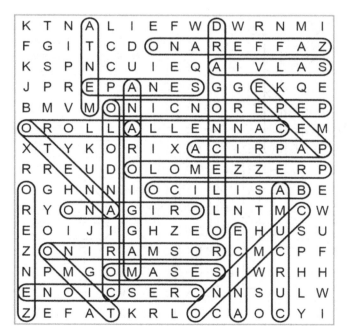

52a – La frutta

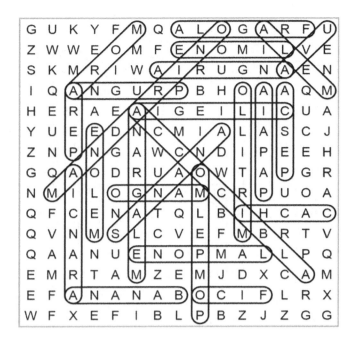

52b – La frutta

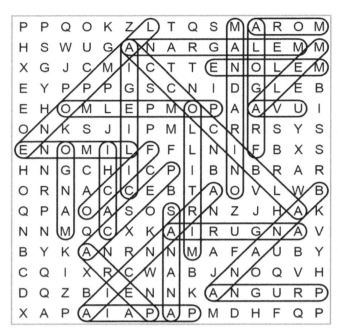

63a – In giardino

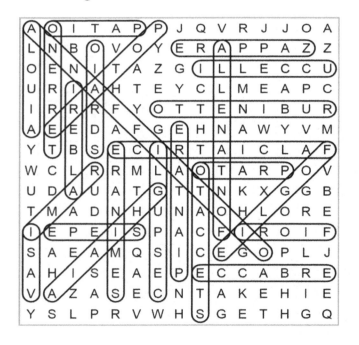

63b – In giardino

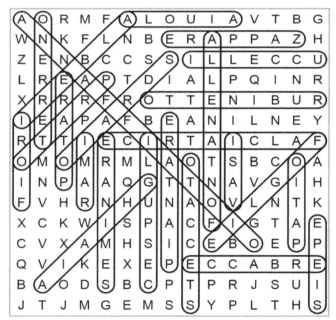

64a – Utensili e accessori da cucina

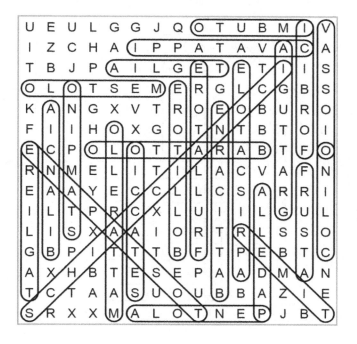

64b – Utensili e accessori da cucina

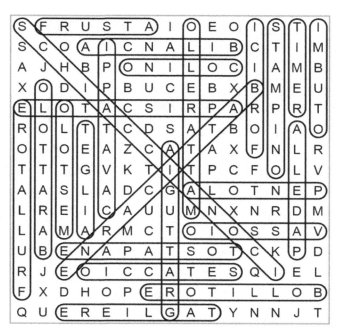

65a – Oggi sposi

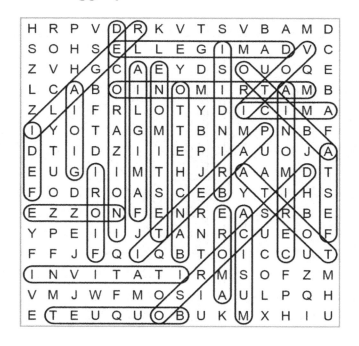

65b – Oggi sposi

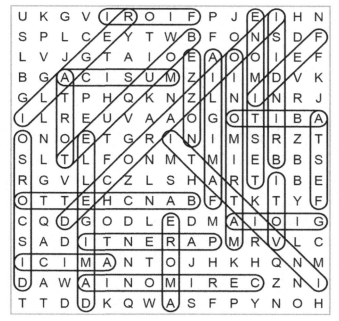

70 – Carnevale

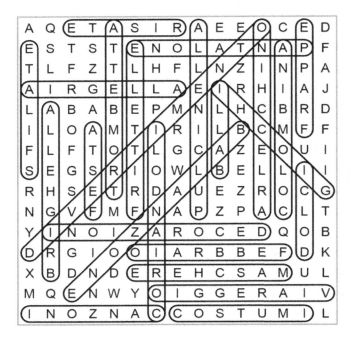

72a – Le carni

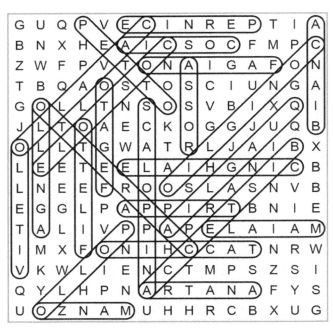

72b – Le carni

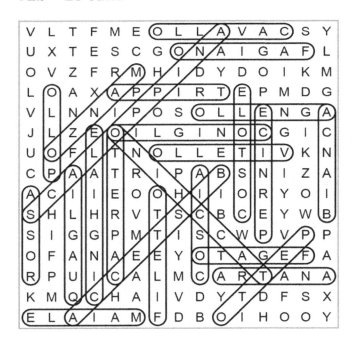

73a – Il pesce

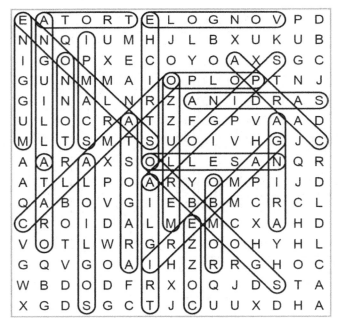

73b – Il pesce

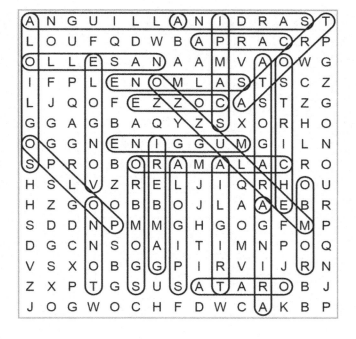

74 – Giochiamo a carte

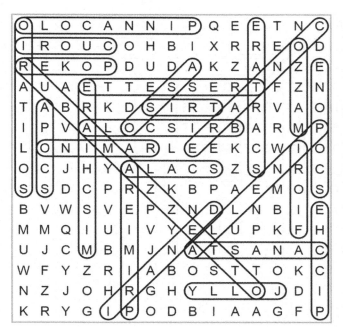

82a – Le verdure

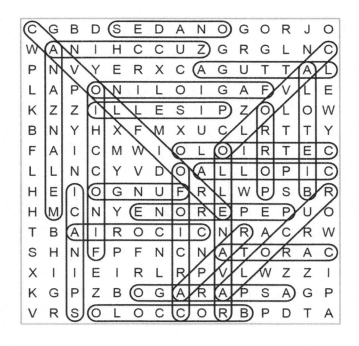

82b – Le verdure

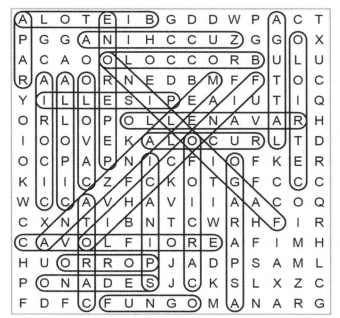

83a – Attività del tempo libero

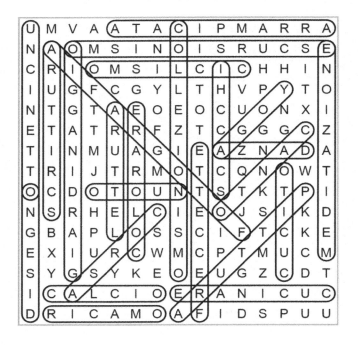

83b – Attività del tempo libero

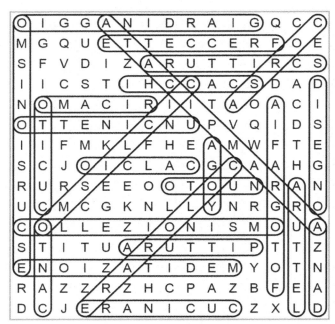

84a – A tavola

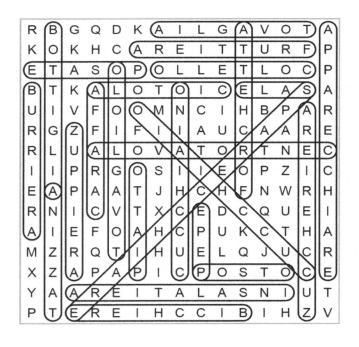

84b – A tavola

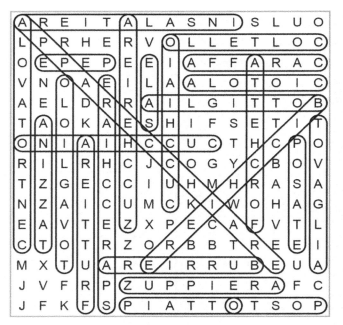

88 – Tipi di pasta

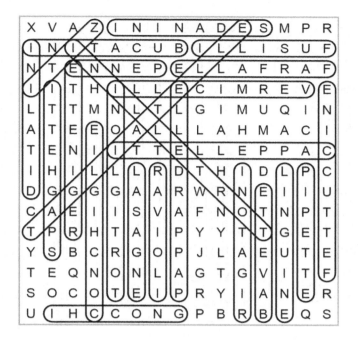

89a – Abbigliamento

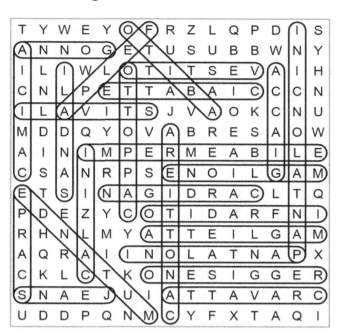

89b – Abbigliamento

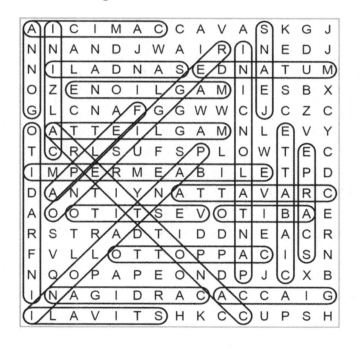

90a – Accessori e gioielli

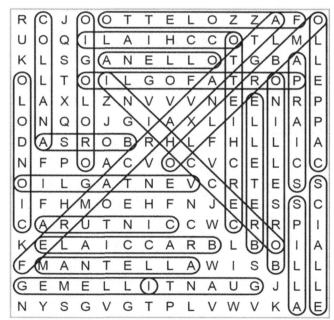

90b – Accessori e gioielli

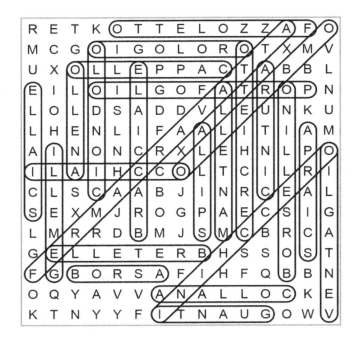

94a – Facciamo le pulizie

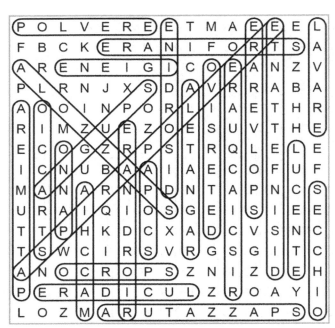

94b – Facciamo le pulizie

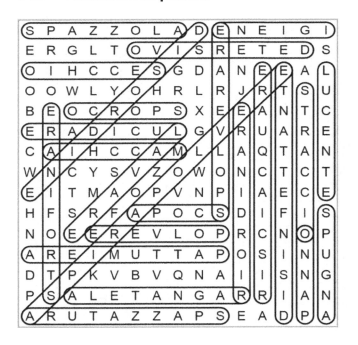

95a – Qualità di un bravo genitore

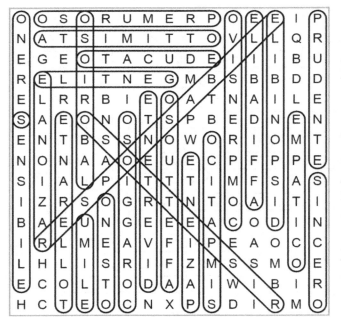

95b – Qualità di un bravo genitore

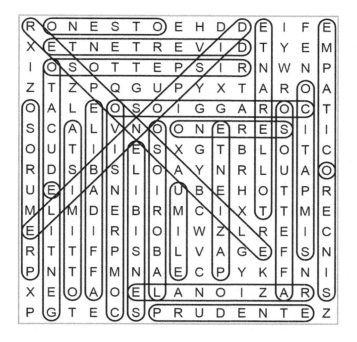

96 – Tipi di dolci

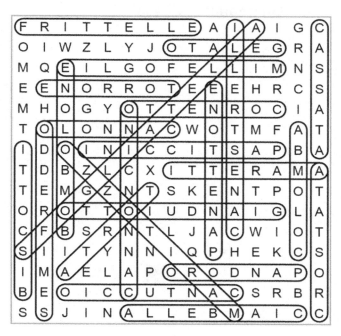

Freeform Crossword Solutions

4 – Un neonato in casa

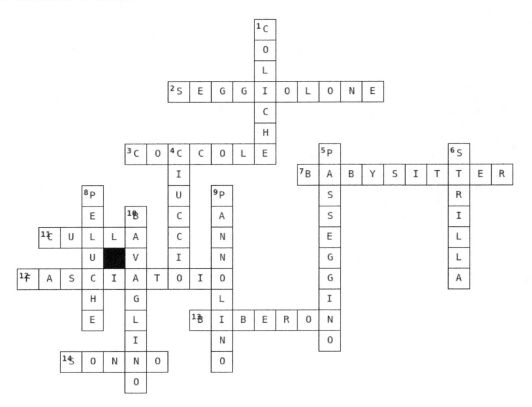

5 – Facciamo colazione

16 – Spaghetti al pomodoro

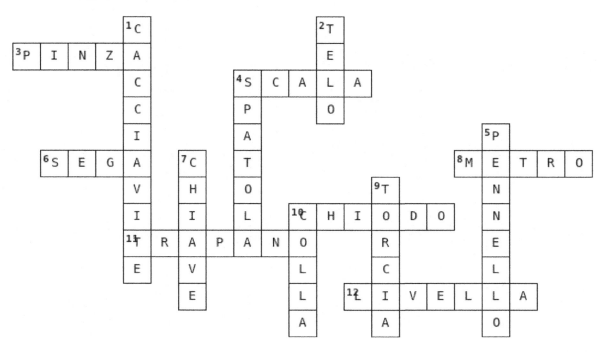

17 – Bricolage/Fai da te

21 – Una passeggiata in centro

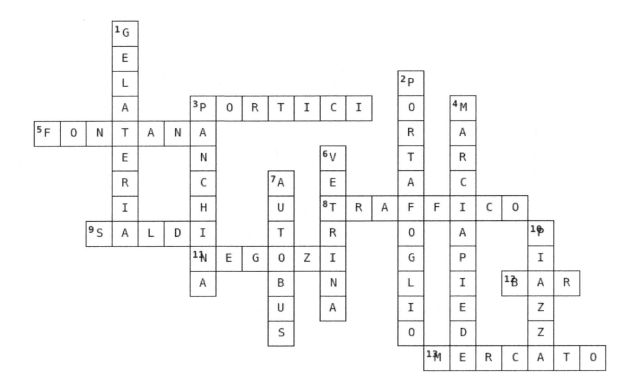

28 – Facciamo una torta

29 – Giochi e giocattoli

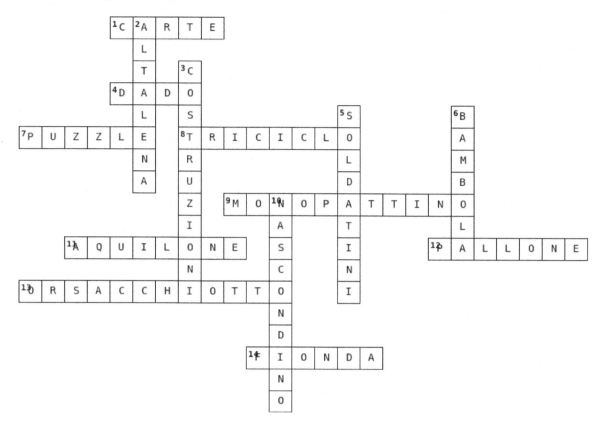

41 – Le belle favole

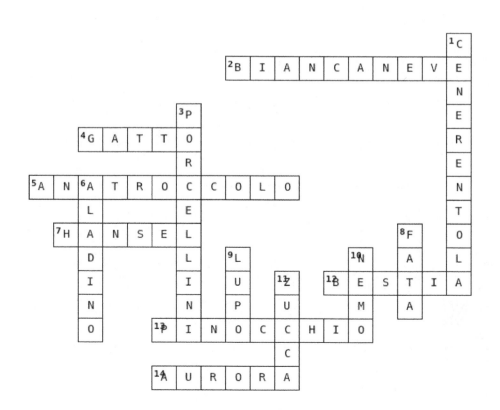

42 – Relazioni di famiglia

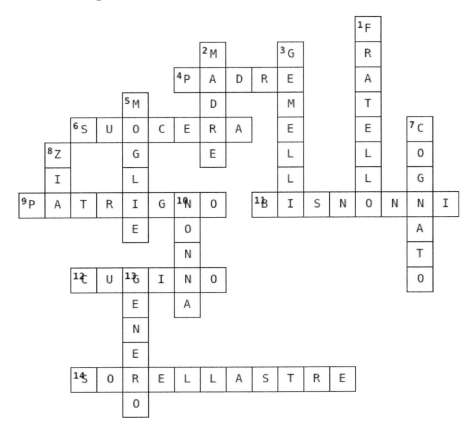

53 – Si va in vacanza

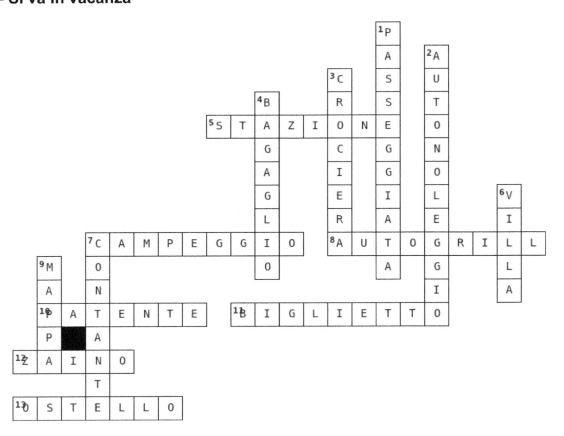

54 – Ora della nanna

66 – Un bel libro

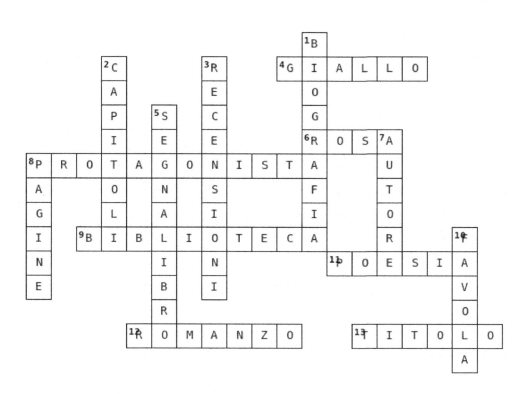

67 – La festa di San Valentino

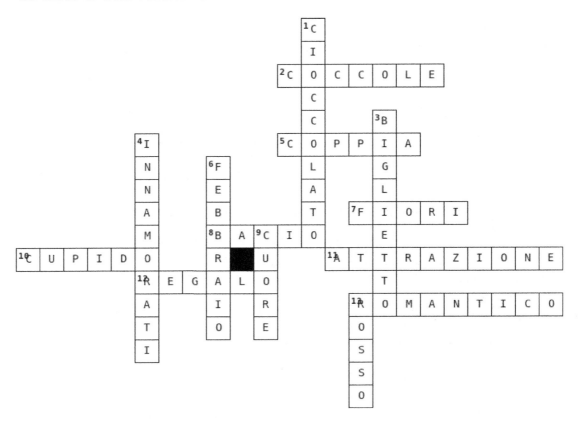

75 – Quando non stiamo bene

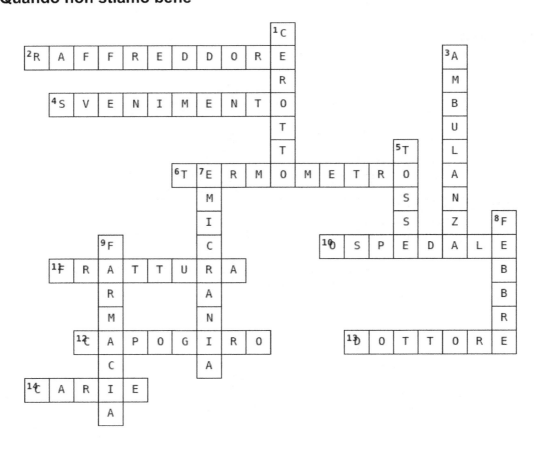

76 – Il primo giorno di scuola (elementare)

80 – La festa di Capodanno

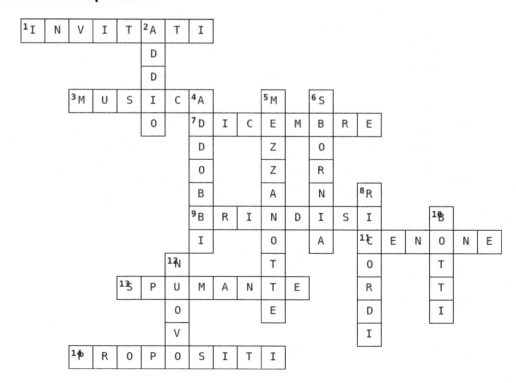

91 – Relax serale

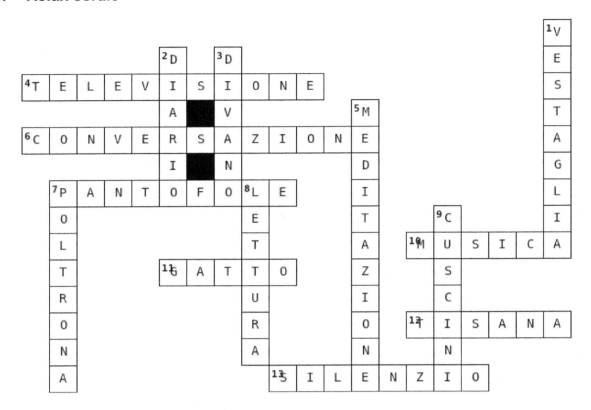

92 – Il trasloco

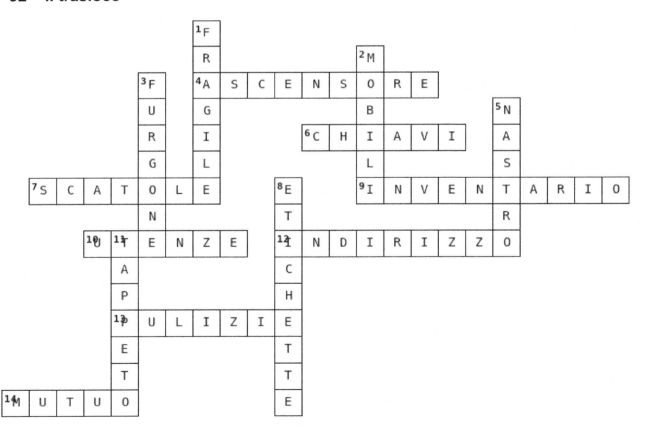

97 – Passatempi

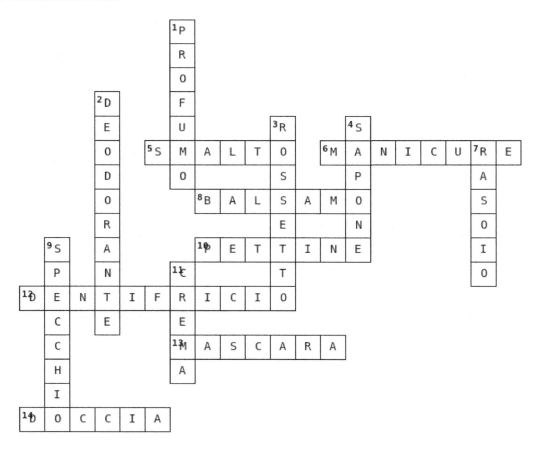

99 – Facciamoci belli

Word Fit Puzzle Solutions

8 – I nonni

9 – Tipi di abitazione

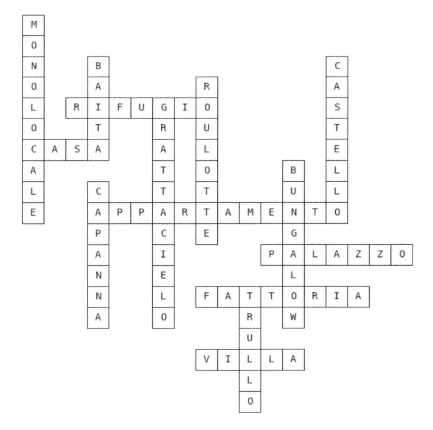

20 – Addio al nubilato/celibato

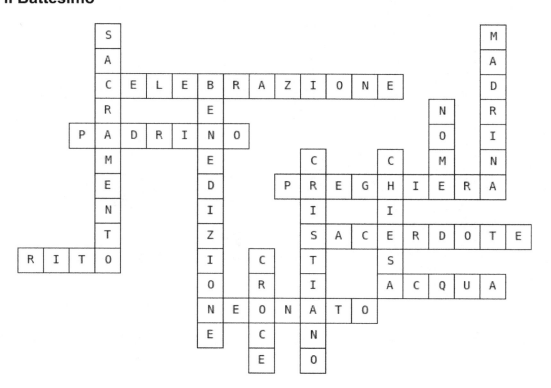

32 – Il Battesimo

33 – L'albero genealogico

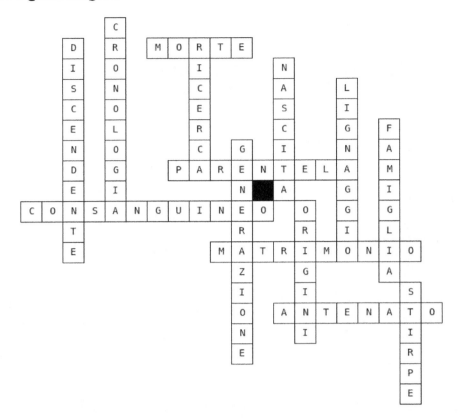

45 – Il bucato

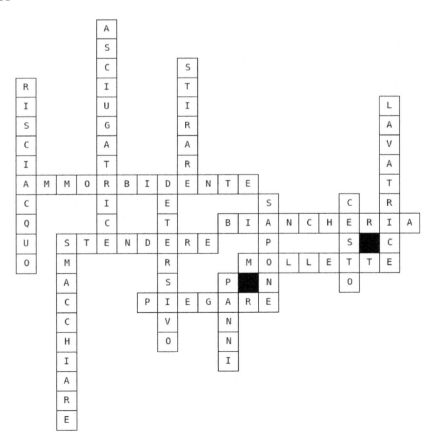

46 – Per una serena convivenza

58 – Articoli di cancelleria

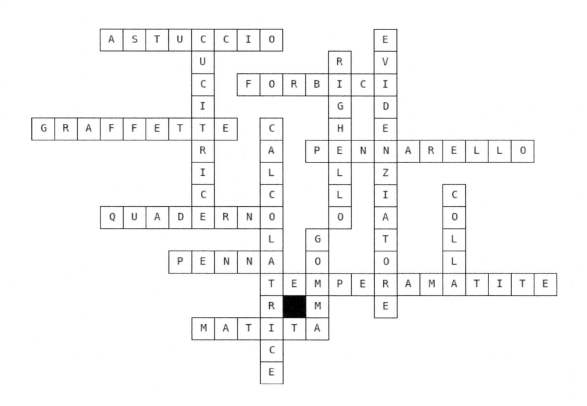

59 – I rumori di casa

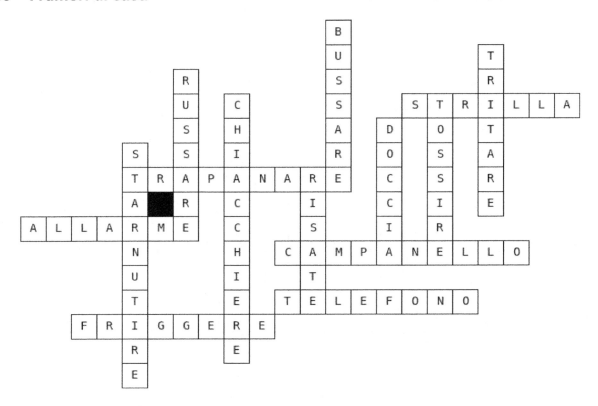

79 – Parti di un capo d'abbigliamento

99 – Una cena con amici

100 – Un funerale in famiglia

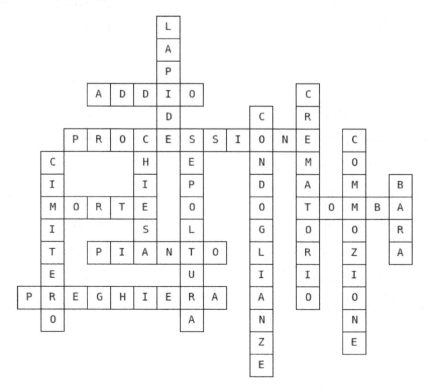

Word Match Solutions

6 – Festa della mamma e del papà

biglietto	→	card
fiori	→	flowers
regalo	→	present
domenica	→	Sunday
ricordi	→	memories
figlio	→	son
figlia	→	daughter
brindisi	→	toast
festa	→	celebration
affetto	→	fondness
famiglia	→	family
fotografia	→	photo

7 – Leggiamo il giornale

titolo	→	headline
articolo	→	article
pagina	→	page
fotografia	→	photo
rubrica	→	column
notizie	→	news
pubblicità	→	advert
vignetta	→	cartoon
edicola	→	newsagent's
intervista	→	interview
stampa	→	press
giornalista	→	journalist

18 – Hobby

lettura	→	libro
pittura	→	pennello
ricamo	→	ago
astronomia	→	telescopio
giardinaggio	→	rastrello
scacchi	→	scacchiera
filatelia	→	francobolli
magia	→	bacchetta
cucina	→	ricettario
maglia	→	ferri
enigmistica	→	cruciverba
danza	→	musica

19 – Attrezzi vari della casa

cacciavite	→	avvitare
metro	→	misurare
forbici	→	tagliare
trapano	→	perforare
torcia	→	illuminare
martello	→	battere
pennello	→	verniciare
ferro	→	stirare
phon	→	asciugare
scopa	→	spazzare
pala	→	spalare
spazzola	→	strofinare

30 – Il vicino di casa antipatico

scorbutico	→	cranky
ficcanaso	→	busybody
maleducato	→	rude
dispettoso	→	spiteful
invadente	→	interfering
chiassoso	→	loud
fastidioso	→	annoying
aggressivo	→	aggressive
litigioso	→	argumentative
brontolone	→	grumbler
indiscreto	→	indiscreet
pettegolo	→	gossipy

31 – Come mostrare amore

abbraccio	→	hug
carezza	→	caress
complimenti	→	compliments
ascolto	→	listening
fiducia	→	trust
onestà	→	honesty
sostegno	→	support
presenza	→	presence
pazienza	→	patience
tenerezza	→	tenderness
affetto	→	affection
rispetto	→	respect

43 – Cucinare

friggere	→	olio
infornare	→	pizza
bollire	→	acqua
mescolare	→	mestolo
tritare	→	coltello
pesare	→	bilancia
apparecchiare	→	tavola
scolare	→	colapasta
frullare	→	uova
insaporire	→	spezie
impanare	→	polpette
scongelare	→	freezer

44 – Sveglia!

sbadiglio	→	sonno
cereali	→	colazione
allarme	→	sveglia
lenzuola	→	letto
luce	→	lampada
cielo	→	alba
barba	→	rasoio
doccia	→	asciugamano
pantofole	→	piedi
indumenti	→	armadio
trucco	→	specchio
fretta	→	ritardo

56 – Pasqua

uova	→	eggs
cioccolato	→	chocolate
pulcino	→	chick
colomba	→	dove
campane	→	bells
agnello	→	lamb
coniglio	→	rabbit
domenica	→	Sunday
risurrezione	→	resurrection
quaresima	→	lent
croce	→	cross
chiesa	→	church

57 – Facciamo i compiti

quaderno	→	notebook
libro	→	book
matita	→	pencil
lezione	→	lesson
ripasso	→	revision
ricerca	→	research
studio	→	study
tema	→	essay
esercizio	→	exercise
lettura	→	reading
penna	→	pen
appunti	→	notes

68 – Abbigliamento e parti del corpo

guanti	→	mani
calzini	→	piedi
pantaloni	→	gambe
reggiseno	→	seno
sciarpa	→	collo
cappello	→	testa
anello	→	dito
trucco	→	viso
bracciale	→	polso
orecchini	→	orecchie
cintura	→	vita
scialle	→	spalle

69 – Dolci e delizie

panettone	→	uvetta
tiramisù	→	mascarpone
amaretti	→	mandorle
gelato	→	latte
crostata	→	marmellata
meringa	→	albumi
cannolo	→	ricotta
babà	→	rum
brownie	→	cioccolato
pasticcini	→	crema
macedonia	→	frutta
cantucci	→	vin santo

77 – Sotto il letto del bambino

mostro	→	monster
calzino	→	sock
briciole	→	crumbs
gatto	→	cat
giocattolo	→	toy
ragno	→	spider
ciabatta	→	slipper
adesivo	→	sticker
disegno	→	drawing
fazzoletto	→	tissue
giornalino	→	comic book
cartacce	→	waste paper

78 – Prendiamoci il tè

teiera	→	teapot
zucchero	→	sugar
biscotti	→	biscuits
torta	→	cake
tazza	→	cup
piattino	→	saucer
cucchiaino	→	teaspoon
infuso	→	brew
latte	→	milk
limone	→	lemon
tovaglioli	→	napkins
vassoio	→	tray

86 – I mostri

dracula	→	vampiro
ciclope	→	gigante
minotauro	→	toro
licantropo	→	lupo
zombie	→	cimitero
mummia	→	bende
strega	→	pozione
fantasma	→	spirito
medusa	→	serpenti
drago	→	fuoco
alieno	→	extraterrestre
cerbero	→	inferi

87 – I versi degli animali

cane	→	abbaia
corvo	→	gracchia
gallo	→	canta
gatto	→	miagola
grillo	→	frinisce
passero	→	cinguetta
piccione	→	tuba
rana	→	gracida
topo	→	squittisce
zanzara	→	ronza
pipistrello	→	stride
gufo	→	gufa

Word Scramble Solutions

12a, 12b – Il ricettario

IINOOPZR	→	PORZIONI
ENIIGTDIENR	→	INGREDIENTI
OCDIEMINNT	→	CONDIMENTI
ZINTRSOUII	→	ISTRUZIONI
UTORACT	→	COTTURA
ENICID	→	INDICE
TETRIAC	→	RICETTA
MTIEP	→	TEMPI
MIAMINGI	→	IMMAGINI
OLCEARI	→	CALORIE
RAUTEATEPMR	→	TEMPERATURA
EPSO	→	PESO

24a, 24b – I compiti di matematica

NTLBELIEA	→	TABELLINE
ZINEDIDAO	→	ADDIZIONE
IVNIOIDES	→	DIVISIONE
OEISATTONRZ	→	SOTTRAZIONE
RNPECAETLUE	→	PERCENTUALE
ZENAROIF	→	FRAZIONE
AEMCIDIL	→	DECIMALI
TMIIECARAT	→	ARITMETICA
UOMERN	→	NUMERO
UASIRM	→	MISURA
ILTLMOUP	→	MULTIPLO
OTGEAERIM	→	GEOMETRIA

36a, 36b – Dolce dormire

IUSCCNO	→	CUSCINO
EOLTT	→	LETTO
NSOOG	→	SOGNO
POORIS	→	RIPOSO
IILNOPSO	→	PISOLINO
NOONS	→	SONNO
ILSNOIZE	→	SILENZIO
ANNANINNNA	→	NINNANANNA
LLAUC	→	CULLA
TQUEIE	→	QUIETE
AASUP	→	PAUSA
NCLLAIEEPHN	→	PENNICHELLA

49a, 49b – Cane e gatto

LROECAL	→	COLLARE
NGILOGAIUZ	→	GUINZAGLIO
AFSU	→	FUSA
ICIOM	→	MICIO
ACINMOAGP	→	COMPAGNIA
OCDA	→	CODA
AMPEZ	→	ZAMPE
OLPE	→	PELO
LOOUICCC	→	CUCCIOLO
IETIVRAOERN	→	VETERINARIO
EONIFL	→	FELINO
IULPC	→	PULCI

55a, 55b – Facciamo merenda

ANPNIO	→	PANINO
LEAMTMLAAR	→	MARMELLATA
TUATRF	→	FRUTTA
TEATL	→	LATTE
OCSCU	→	SUCCO
OSBTTIIC	→	BISCOTTI
DUINBO	→	BUDINO
OGYTUR	→	YOGURT
LRUOFATL	→	FRULLATO
ERLECAI	→	CEREALI
OTATR	→	TORTA
KRREACC	→	CRACKER

62a, 62b – Sul balcone

IGRHIEANR	→	RINGHIERA
ATISV	→	VISTA
EPTNIA	→	PIANTE
OIIFR	→	FIORI
IALTNOVO	→	TAVOLINO
IESED	→	SEDIE
XLRAE	→	RELAX
RIODSA	→	SDRAIO
OSENTIITDO	→	STENDITOIO
ERISTAGTA	→	SIGARETTA
TPCRONERAEE	→	PORTACENERE
OPREATTAP	→	PARAPETTO

71a, 71b – Alcune materie di scuola

TALIONAI	→	ITALIANO
TOSARI	→	STORIA
CSAFEREN	→	FRANCESE
FIREAGOGA	→	GEOGRAFIA
IMAMACTEAT	→	MATEMATICA
IITDTOR	→	DIRITTO
MAIICHC	→	CHIMICA
SOOFIIAFL	→	FILOSOFIA
ICIFSA	→	FISICA
GEESLIN	→	INGLESE
OLGIEEINR	→	RELIGIONE
OILIGAOB	→	BIOLOGIA

81a, 81b – Legumi e frutta secca

IECLTHNICE	→	LENTICCHIE
GAOIIFL	→	FAGIOLI
ECIC	→	CECI
AFVE	→	FAVE
IEPLLIS	→	PISELLI
ICRDIAHA	→	ARACHIDI
CDARNAAI	→	ANACARDI
AEGTCASN	→	CASTAGNE
ONPILI	→	PINOLI
HSICICPAT	→	PISTACCHI
OLICCEON	→	NOCCIOLE
ANELDROM	→	MANDORLE

85a, 85b – L'ufficio in casa

VIAINRSAC	→	SCRIVANIA
IEDSA	→	SEDIA
UTCEOMRP	→	COMPUTER
NTAPATESM	→	STAMPANTE
LNTFOEOE	→	TELEFONO
AERTISAT	→	TASTIERA
MRCHSOE	→	SCHERMO
LEACARTL	→	CARTELLA
ISTRAETSCEA	→	CASSETTIERA
AOCREIDALN	→	CALENDARIO
HBCECAA	→	BACHECA
RLLENAIEACC	→	CANCELLERIA

93a, 93b – Una brava babysitter

TLENAPUU	→	PUNTUALE
FTEASUFTAO	→	AFFETTUOSA
ACIIPSTMA	→	SIMPATICA
EVDRTEENIT	→	DIVERTENTE
USARPROEM	→	PREMUROSA
TETTAAN	→	ATTENTA
FAFLABIEDI	→	AFFIDABILE
AZEEPTNI	→	PAZIENTE
OPMIRCNEVAS	→	COMPRENSIVA
AAPCCE	→	CAPACE
TLAIBADTEA	→	ADATTABILE
SOAETN	→	ONESTA

Cryptogram Solutions

10 – Quote by Oliver Wendell Holmes Sr.

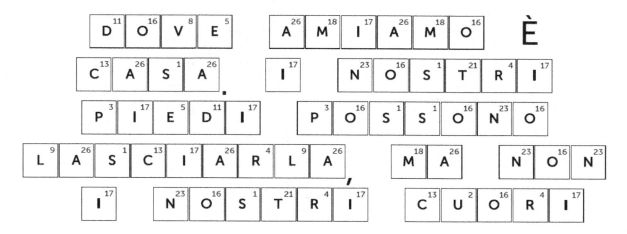

D O V E   A M I A M O   È
C A S A .   I   N O S T R I
P I E D I   P O S S O N O
L A S C I A R L A ,   M A   N O N
I   N O S T R I   C U O R I

Translation: Where we love is home, home that our feet may leave, but not our hearts.

---

11 – Quote by Christian Morgenstern

L A   C A S A   N O N   È
D O V E   V I V I   M A
D O V E   T I
C A P I S C O N O

Translation: Home is not where you live, but where they understand you.

22 – Quote by Michel de Montaigne

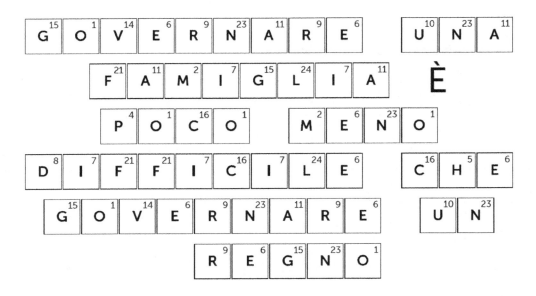

Translation: There is little less trouble in governing a family than a whole kingdom.

---

23 – Quote by Johann Wolfgang von Goethe

Translation: He is happiest, be he king or peasant, who finds peace in his home.

34 – Quote by Unknown

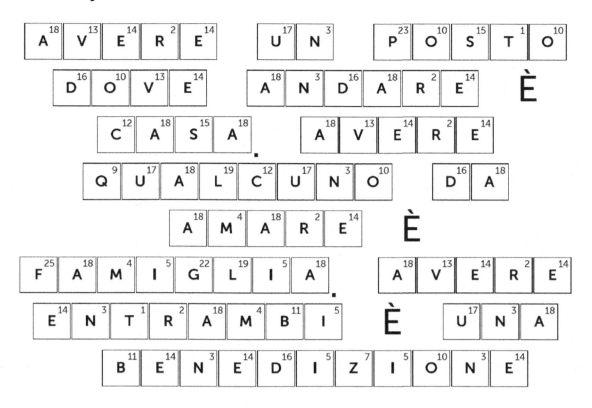

Translation: Having somewhere to go is home, having someone to love is family, having both is a blessing.

---

35 – Quote by Ralph Waldo Emerson

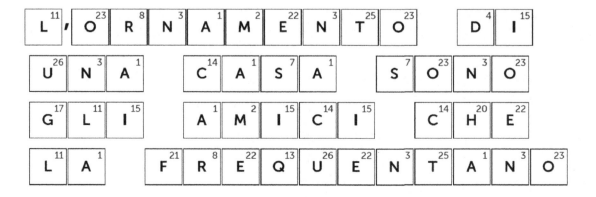

Translation: The ornament of a house is the friends who frequent it.

47 – Quote by Leo Tolstoy

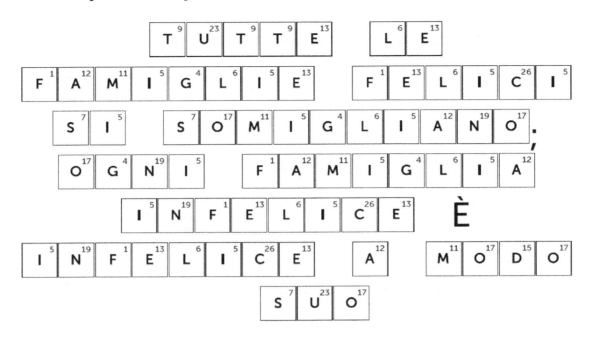

Translation: All happy families are alike; each unhappy family is unhappy in its own way.

---

48 – Quote by Benjamin Franklin

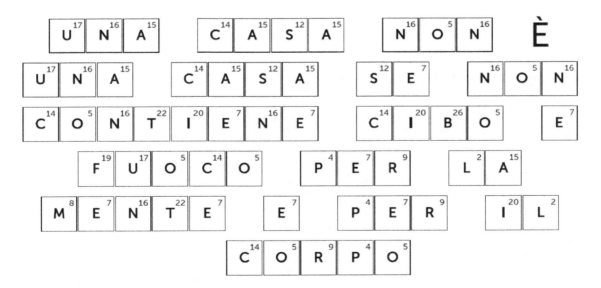

Translation: A house is not a home unless it contains food and fire for the mind as well as the body.

60 – Quote by George Augustus Moore

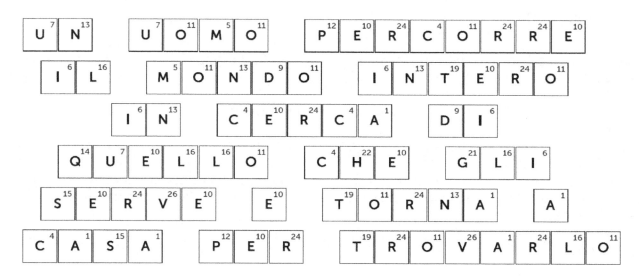

Translation: A man travels the world over in search of what he needs and returns home to find it.

61 – Quote by Henry David Thoreau

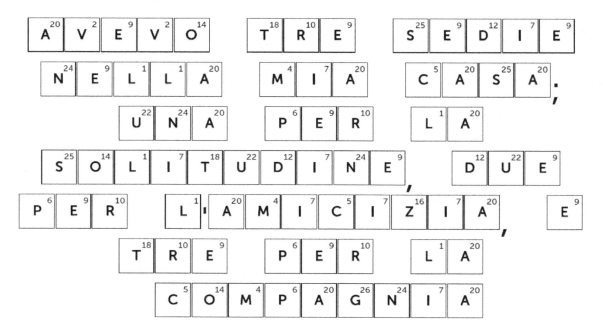

Translation: I had three chairs in my house; one for solitude, two for friendship, three for society.

Note from the author

I hope you enjoyed solving the puzzles in this book and that these helped you learn a few Italian words too.

As an independent author, I don't receive funding from government, corporations or charities.
So I am indebted to my loyal readers (like you) for spreading the word about my work.

If you've enjoyed this book, I'd be grateful if you would spend a couple of minutes leaving your review on Amazon. Don't worry about how long it is. Even a short review makes a huge difference.

Grazie di cuore

Martina

Made in United States
North Haven, CT
22 November 2021

11411635R00098